PASTORAL MUSIC
IN PRACTICE
2

Children, Liturgy, and Music

Edited by Virgil C. Funk

The Pastoral Press
Washington, D.C.

ISBN: 0-912405-73-2
© The Pastoral Press, 1990
All Rights Reserved

The Pastoral Press
225 Sheridan Street, NW
Washington, D.C. 20011
(202) 723-1254

The Pastoral Press is the publications division of the National
Association of Pastoral Musicians, a membership organization of
musicians and clergy dedicated to fostering the art of musical
liturgy.

Printed in the United States of America

CONTENTS

Music Education: Foundation for a Singing Community

INTRODUCTION

The 1973 Directory for Masses with Children* initiated a new era of liturgical development in the Roman Catholic Church. Continuing Vatican II's desire that all the members of the assembly "as far as possible easily understand and take part in the rites fully and actively" (Constitution on the Sacred Liturgy, no. 21), the Directory calls on all parish communities to "help children readily and joyfully to encounter Christ together in the eucharistic celebration" (no. 54).

The National Association of Pastoral Musicians through its conventions, its journal *Pastoral Music,* and through various resources available from The Pastoral Press, has endeavored to offer parish leadership the means whereby to stimulate liturgical celebrations that allow children to celebrate their own faith and, by so doing, to be gradually incorporated into the celebration of the adult community. For children to celebrate well, it is not a matter of employing gimmicks and other devices which well-intentioned adults at times tend to think appropriate for the young. The task at hand is to celebrate rituals which, in their simplicity and beauty, engage the imaginative and creative powers of the young so that they might experience the loving Lord present among them. To do so requires an understanding on the part of adults charged with preparing liturgies for children. At stake is an understanding as to the meaning of liturgy, its elements and dynamics, its presuppositions and requirements. As an aid to acquiring these insights, we have gathered into this volume various articles that have appeared throughout the years in *Pastoral Music.* Included are both visionary as well as "nuts and bolts" approaches.

Leaders of children's celebrations need a basic understanding of what liturgy in general is all about. Accordingly, the volume begins with two foundational articles on participation by an assembly that is truly alive. Several articles are included on the implications of the Directory for Masses with Children. Children's choirs, so important if we are to improve the musical participation of future generations of worshipers, are then treated. Finally, music education in the parish is considered from several perspectives.

Improving the quality of a parish's worship life requires understanding, hard work, a sense of humor, and patience. Overnight accomplishments are often ephemeral. Needed is a long-term commitment toward a goal. What is true for worship by the adult community is no less true for worship by our children.

Virgil C. Funk

*Throughout this volume reference is often made to the Directory for Masses with Children. This document, issued by the Congregation for Divine Worship, may be ordered from the USCC Publishing Services, 3241 Fourth Street, N.E., Washington, DC 20017-1194. The Directory is also reprinted toward the front of the sacramentary or missal.

The Community
Alive and Participating

John Melloh

ONE

THE PRAYER OF PARTICIPATION

The heavenly musicians had been practicing for eons of years; the celestial poets had framed, revised, and polished their texts for the ten millionth time; supernal choirs finally had their harmonies perfectly blended, each of the billions of voices was perfectly in balance; the ethereal harps had been finely tuned, the incense bowls filled to the brimming-full, the white robes had been washed in the blood of the lamb, and they were marvelous in brilliance, the starry crowns polished to a wonderful gleam. All was ready.

Flashes of lightning shot through the heavens; peals of thunder sounded; lighted torches burned brightly and the four living creatures began with their unceasing song, night and day, praising: "Holy, holy, holy is the Lord God Almighty." The twenty-four elders bowed down before the one who sits on the throne, proclaiming: "O Lord and God, you are worthy to receive glory and honor and power." Incense filled the hallowed courts and new songs rang through the air: "You, O Lamb of God, are worthy to take the scroll and break open its seal." Tens of thousands of angels, the four living creatures, and the elders formed the choir and sang at the top of their lungs: "The Lamb who was slain is worthy to receive power, wealth, wisdom and strength, honor, glory and praise." And *this* celestial schola was joined by every creature in heaven, on earth, and in the world below, chanting: "Prasie and glory, and might forever!" The living creatures resounded with cries of "Amen." And the elders fell down and worshipped.

This continued night and day—this heavenly delight, this spectacular collage of sight, sound, and song. This worship of the Lamb was a real feast of participation and the divine scenario places before our poetic imaginations a vision of the ethos, the spirit of true worship of the Lamb. Acclamations, sung dialogues, attentive listening, ritual gestures—all combined in a cosmic act of praise to the Lamb (Rev 4-5; cf. Feuillet, *The Apocalypse*).

Let us leave this scene and return to the terrestrial, lest our supernal visions turn into mere flights of fancy. But let us hold on to this vision of feast, of paschal mystery, of community, of participation.

"My cursory survey of liturgical literature produced since the Council," declared Aidan Kavanagh, "reveals that little has been said over the past ten years about the matter of participation, except for repeating Council maxims" (Kavanagh, p. 343). Kavanagh was right in 1973; I believe that he is right today. It may be sheer arrogance on my part, but I shall attempt to say something about the prayer of participation without merely repeating the council maxims.

I would like to examine the notion of participation in the wider sense of sharing in the Christian mystery of Jesus' dying and rising and then focus specifically on the participation of the assembly in the eucharist.

The topic, "The Prayer of Participation," involves the dynamic relationship of community prayer and community participation—both exciting and extensive notions. To treat this topic is not dissimilar from the mating of two whales: it is a vast undertaking. Thus, my remarks will, of necessity, not be the last word on participation but will provide a framework, through sketching out the main lines of this liturgical turf, in order to spur your own creative reflection on the topic.

PARTICIPATION: SHARING IN THE DYING AND RISING OF JESUS

This is the first question: Participation in what? To restrict participation to the assembly's role in eucharistic celebration is to take an incorrect starting point. Participation in the eucharistic event is an outcome, not a genesis point (Kavanagh, p. 45). Thus, participation for the Christian must be viewed in a wider dimension—the life of faith. The only object of Christian faith is the mystery of Jesus dead and risen. It is a mystery that exists in different modalities: it is prefigured in the Old Testament; it is historically accomplished in the earthly life of Jesus; it is ritually celebrated in the sacraments; it is mystically present in the inner depths of the believer; it is socially accomplished in the church on earth, and it is eschatologically realized in the heavenly kingdom (Daniélou, p. 17).

Participation for us Christians is in the totality of life—the fullness of living in Jesus. "It is now not I that live, but Christ lives in me." To share in this life of Jesus is to live a full human life, a human life that is divinized because of the gratuity of a loving God. Thus, to be a Christian is to be fully alive and this is, as Irenaeus suggests, the glory of God.

The Christian life is an adventure of faith; it is a journey toward fullness of being. It is a journey undertaken by the individual, but not embarked upon alone. To participate in the journey, the Christian must experience the gift of God as an individual person and as a person deeply immersed in a community of faith.

To believe in Jesus—to have faith—is to have eternal life; not a light at the end of a tunnel, but a light seen in the darkness. To believe in Jesus is not to have the lonely empty place, the void, the abyss filled magically, but it is to allow oneself to be possessed by the Presence of the Holy One.

Each Christian is, in truth, a shaman—a God-invaded person, filled with the fire of the Spirit of Vision and Truth and with the light that shines forth from the tomb. But to be God-invaded is to experience the deepness, the uncertainty, the un-comfort of the tomb, the emptiness, the darkness—and in this experience to know that there is a sure hope of salvation in that very moment. The transformation of our lives is possible only through sacrifice and surrender—surrender through a process of conversion that focuses the mystery of living on the cross that leads to final resurrection.

The Christian life becomes merely a cognitive blueprint for an *ersatz* existence, a substitute for living, an ecclesiastical bromide, unless it is enacted as a way of life in common. The Christian exists within a community or not at all. The vine and branches business, the crop full of tares, the wedding banquet imagery are glimpses into how the mystery is to be lived: in community with others.

Life in Christian community is more than an Esalon group, much more than a touchy-feely experience that leads to warm fuzzies, much more than automated responses of everyone after the fashion of Artoo Detoo. "Christian community, then, is primarily an experience of sharing God's love realized in each person (Seasoltz, p. 114). It is the sharing of the real-ized (that is, made real) love of God that touches the heart of each believer in such a way that it must be communicated. It is the outpouring of a Spirit that removes us from isolation and alienation and creates a reconciled community.

In short, the Christian life is a life in Jesus, an adventure of conversion, an ongoing, never-ceasing experience of dying and rising with Jesus in each of us and in each of us as part of a community that stands a light to the world and judges the world by the criteria of the Gospel. In order to participate in this common way of life, each person must really belong to the community, lest the sharing in the life of the community be only a pious phrase, lest having a part in the community degenerate into a placing of cold hard cash in computerized envelopes, attending woodenly a stale liturgical exercise here and there, and perhaps baking a Duncan Hines package cake for the parish bake sale.

A real sharing of life implies sharing of the vision, that insight into the ever self-realizing Kingdom and the Presence of the Holy One. It is putting on of a new world view. Without this change in perspective—viewing the world through gospel-colored glasses and not merely rose-tinted contact lenses—an individual does not really belong, but stands on the very fringe of the Christian enterprise.

A great emphasis has been placed on the *de facto* restoration of awe-inspiring initiatory rites. And rightly so. For this process is the one that forges Christians, under the aegis of the Spirit and the Spirit's heavy workload of operating through us partially-reconstructed Christians. (Thanks be to God that the Spirit does not tire easily.) Not born, but made, Tertullian said: this is how we become Christian. Made through genuine prayer, that real cry of the invading spirit within us, made through fasting (and not just Scarsdale diets), made through almsgiving till it really hurts the pocketbook (and not just because of Alfred Kahn's policies), made through sacrifice, that total giving of ourselves, our persons to one another in love. "To be a prayerful person [converted] is to stand in the power and presence of God, but it is also to have a presence that should be powerful in the presence of other people [community]" (Seasoltz, p. 119). Our own conversion in the midst of community is contagious. The experience of Jesus' dying and rising is communicated much like a disease: through social contact.

So far, I have suggested that participation, first of all, refers to dying and rising with Jesus. This experience also happens to us individually, but as individuals in a real community. This is the foundation for liturgical participation.

Tom Talley, in his own inimitable way, epitomized the role of celebration: for life to be lively, it must be celebrated. This is what the Christian adventure is: lively, full of life, a swallowing of the existential soup without straining out even the okra. It is joy-suffused celebration in the tension of the already and the not-yet, in the shadow of the cross, that shadow produced by the shining rays of the Son of Justice who has conquered sin and ultimate death.

For Christians to be alive, they need to pray and to play. The adventure of faith is far from grim: it is prayerful, playful existence. To play is not to assume an ostrich-like posture, but to confront the dynamism of daily living with confidence that the victory is ours. Celebration is nothing more and nothing else than ritualized play. It runs the gamut from parish-sponsored pot-luck suppers, bazzars and picnics, yes, even budget meetings, to liturgical celebration in which we offer our fragile human-and-thus-divine service to the Lord in assembly.

The outcome of bearing in our bodies the marks of the Crucified, the outcome of our faith adventure, the outcome of faithfull living is full-blown eucharistic celebration: a sharing in this sacrificial meal that eloquently speaks to us of the new age and new vision with which we are gifted and which we share. Authentic eucharistic celebration is possible only as an outcome of ongoing participation in the dying and rising of Jesus. Those who come to the Table of the Lord do so because a symbol-making community lives out of what is articulated in celebration. The eucharistic celebration is one of celebrative storytelling and playful ritualizing, which presupposes the radical presence of God in the world and engages the community in the event-ualizing (that is, making into an event) of the pervasive presence of the God of mystery and fullness of life.

Celebration demands community. You just can't celebrate alone. A birthday party celebrated in isolation cannot be a birthday party. And the foundation for celebration is a shared experience. Deep experiences in an individual's life move one to share the experiences. Grief at the death of a friend, profound joy at the birth of a child, happiness over a promotion, sorrow at the loss of a job—all these experiences move us to share the events. The human spirit longs for communal ritualization of real events.

The eucharist, as a celebration, requires community. Our experiences of Jesus dying and rising, revealed in the love of a husband and wife, manifested in the reconciliation of a family, manifested in our developing realization of selfhood—all these experiences move us to give thanks and praise to God and to do so in the midst of assembly.

The eucharist, as celebration, demands the participation of those who assist at it. This ritualization is of the collective sacrifice of Christ, for he is the head, and all humanity is recapitulated in him. Were the eucharist only the repetition or renewal of Calvary, there would be no theological justification for participation (Roguet, p. 122). The participants would only have to contemplate a past sacrifice, benefit from it, and give thanks. But the sacramentality of eucharist extends beyond the historical. "Do this in memory of me" stands in contrast with a unique historical and metaphysical unrepeatable event. The once for all sacrifice of Jesus is truly once for all.

But the sacrament is a sanctifying action of a people; it is a symbol-action taken up actively by those for whom it is intended—the holy people won by the blood of Christ. It is a well-known maxim of Augustine: God has redeemed us without our cooperation, but God will not sanctify us without our cooperation. To experience the dying and rising of Jesus in sacramental activity is a possibility resting on our activity of making eucharist. And this wonder-filled activity is not restricted to any one category of Christians, but belongs *de facto* and *de jure* to the assembly as a whole.

If the eucharist is the banquet of the Kingdom and is an irruption of Kingdom in time, then the people of the Kingdom must act. If it is a banquet, then we must dine. If it is the meal of the Kingdom, then we must share the Kingdom with one another. If it is a symbol-making event, then we must become the very symbols that speak. If it is sacrificial meal, then we ourselves must sacrifice, making ourselves holy through allowing the life and death of Jesus to be the life and death of us all. Participating in this meal means we must pay attention to the analog of meal-sharing in our lives. To share a meal is to be present to the event. It is to share food and drink, diaphanous symbols of life-sharing. It is the offering and accepting of what sustains life and sustains life in common. Sharing a meal demands presence; it means, for example, that we are not staring at the TV; it means not politely staring at the food. It is dining at a common table that reveals the stake we have in one another's living.

Our eucharistic celebration is "valid" in the same way that meals are "valid." If they are celebrations of my life and my life with others, if they are celebrations of my life in communion with yours, if they are celebrations of the death and resurrection of Jesus, not metaphorically, but real-ly, then they are valid.

"Active participation is the right of the Christian and a duty imposed with the force of truth" (Neunhauser, p. 109). Before 1920, the active participation of the assembly was all but ignored. The priest was isolated experientially from the community gathered for prayer, the servers performed perfunctorily official duties, and the faithful engaged in a contemplation of a distant mystery, especially through interior communion. While the principle that the entire church, head and members (*Mediator Dei*), offers the eucharist as the chosen race of royal priesthood was never denied in theory, it was a hidden reality in practice.

Aggiornamento—the cry raised by Vatican II—sought to reconcile liturgical practice with liturgical theory. If life in the church is an act of praise seen as preparation for worship and as consequence of worship, and if the worship act itself is not viewed as the making real of this life through celebrative articulation, then there is no need to participate in eucharist. If the eucharist, however, is a real liturgical offering, the outcome of a style of living and the sustenance of this lifestyle, then there must be participation of all—because who but the community can posit the eucharistic act?

"Judging from the quality of participation in the liturgical event, it appears that we have a classic instance of a truth becoming a truism, a truism becoming an unexamined assumption, and an unexamined assumption becoming a fixed, ideological mindset that often has less to do with the nature of liturgy than with some immature cleric's fantasy life. Liturgical participation in such a circumstance degenerates into a wordy and mawkish egalitarianism, relevant, for the most part, to social action or psycho-therapy rather than to gospel. Participation becomes its antithesis" (Kavanagh, p. 344).

Up to this point I have avoided any precision concerning the term "participation." Noah Webster, come to the rescue! Participation means: (1) to possess something of the nature of a person, thing, or quality; (2) to take part; (3) to have a part or share in something.

"To possess something of the nature of a person, thing, or quality" refers, in our case, to the foundational element of participation: the dying and rising of Jesus in which we all share through conversion, epitomized in the sacraments of initiation.

"To take part" or "to have a part or share in something" implies this same foundational element, but speaks to us of the modes of participating in eucharist; each of us and all of us have special roles or parts in a common activity. "To take part" means to express ownership of the event—to express my own commitment to the event and to reveal the communal stewardship of the assembly. "To have a share in" implies the coordination of various liturgical roles that are the assembly's. "To have a share or part in" means to outlaw deviant forms of participation: on the one extreme, that style of celebration in which the presiding minister does just about everything for a group of somewhat interested spectators, who persist in doing their individualized thing; and the other extreme, that style of celebration in which everyone is expected to do everything. Neither extreme is revelatory of a mainline concept of the church; both throw their lot in with the eccentric (that is, lacking central focus) ecclesiologies. Both extremes deny to the assembly its rightful place: on the one hand, the assembly becomes a group of tableau viewers, isolated in excessive interiority; on the other hand, the assembly becomes bearers of unqualified exuberance, lacking both grace and flair.

Vatican II boldly stated the traditional principle that "all the faithful be led to that full, conscious and active participation in liturgical celebrations which is demanded by the very nature of the liturgy" (no. 14).

Let us un-pick the council maxim. "Full" participation can mean nothing else than the sharing in the salvific mystery of Christ. Our participation is "full" only because as a Christian people we share in the one *leitourgia*, the life of Christ Jesus. We are plunged into this mystery through Christian initiation and share in the one passage, the one pascha of Jesus, his *transitus*-from flesh-condition to spirit-condition. To speak of "full" participation, in my mind, has nothing to do with quantitative approaches to the question. Nor does fullness relate just to liturgy; it relates to celebration insofar as this common prayer flows from a life shared.

"Conscious" participation impinges on the foundational. To share consciously means to recognize that we, as persons, are enspirited fleshes or enfleshed-spirits. It is to take quite seriously the incarnation as a principle for living; the flesh reveals the spirit and the spirit is embodied in the flesh. Not assenting to this principle is to run the risk of creating the anomalous situation of a liturgy divorced from life experiences. Consciousness of who we are in our daily living implies conscious realization of who are are in celebration. To borrow a lovely phrase from T.S. Eliot:

> These are only hints and guesses
> hints followed by guesses; and the rest
> is prayer, observance, discipline,
>   thought and action.
> The hint half-guessed, the gift half-
>   understood,
> is Incarnation.
>   (The Dry Salvages, 11. 212-215)

"Active participation" again speaks of the foundational, the appropriating of the mystery each moment of the day. And in the celebrative assembly, we attend to the mystery through our activity of symbol-making in a context of prayer and praise. Participation, I wish to suggest, eventualizes the foundation reality of the mystery of Jesus by giving that mystery concrete symbolic expression. Participation is about activating the mystery, not thinking about the mystery; participation is about performing the mystery, not assenting to the truth of the mystery; participation is about being the mystery together with one another, not idly gazing at a mystery far-distant from ourselves.

Abhishiktanada is right: there are no part-time Christian contemplatives; each Christian is a contemplative who savors the mystery in its expression. Contemplation is about devotion, giving expression to the bond that exists because of the Father's gift in Christ Jesus, and not about disconnected moments of heightened awareness (Abhishiktanada, Ch. 1).

In sum, I have suggested that there are two basic modes of participation and the two are really one: sharing in the mystery of Jesus in our lifestyle, and expressing this life preeminently in the liturgical act. Enough has been said about the former. I shall concentrate on the latter.

PARTICIPATING IN LITURGY

Within the Christian celebration, there is a diversity of parts to be played. We have a share in the performance of these parts. Unless there is an articulation and coordination of the various parts or roles, the celebration suffers, even to the point of becoming its antithesis.

The modalities of participation that I shall examine are the following: verbal, musical, visual-spatial, dramatic, ritual, silent.

We all remember the Baltimore Catechism's admonition to assist at Mass with "reverence, attention, and devotion." This still holds true today. Reverence is for the life that we share in common; attention is to the mystery in our life and in our celebration; and devotion is the expression of faith. No faith really exists that is not expressed. And it is here that the apparent dichotomy between performance and participation disappears. When we realize that it is only through worthy performance that participatory roles are enacted, and that it is only through worthy performance that the symbol-making function of the community is actualized, that the mystery is enfleshed in our world, then the dichotomy vanishes. Our prayer occurs in the concrete, in the expressed-reality, or it does not occur.

Verbal participation. Liturgy is an experience of the *Word* as real and relevant to us. It is more than mere human words, but our religious experience is expressed verbally at times. Verbal participation that we have in eucharist takes the form of proclamation and response; the initial greeting and response, which Augustine himself sees as constitutive of the community, the resounding Amen to presidential prayers, the full-throated proclamation of the Creed—all are verbal.

True, the responses are fixed, rather than spontaneous, but so are football cheers and chants. The fixity can militate against our *feeling* that the responses are genuine, but once we are caught up in the event, the responses bear the personal stamp of inner spirit.

Musical participation. For the assembly to respond to the readings with responsorial chants, to acclaim the gospel with a vigorous and uplifting Alleluia, to punctuate the eucharistic prayer enthusiastically with a resounding Holy, Memorial Acclamation, and Great Amen is to express our dying and rising with Jesus; it is to attend to the mystery present. For the assembly to dialogue musically with the choir and cantor and one with another in various musical forms is to express the unity that exists within the diversity of our participatory roles.

Visual-spatial participation. The sadder but wiser liturgist knows how visual participation can denature the liturgical act. Participation through seeing only had led to faulty theologizing about the eucharist. Merely watching the priest and his ritual actions is not considered the norm for celebration.

Liturgy takes place in time and space. To participate actively requires a oneness with our space. Worshiping the Father in spirit and in truth is either facilitated or hindered by our space. Trying to celebrate the eucharist when waist-high in wood is a difficult proposition; orienting our worship space so that it resembles a lecture hall is to make an unfortunate statement about participation. We need to take seriously the Federal Aviation Administration's collision avoidance principle: See and be seen.

We need to see one another: praising, making music, listening in profound silence, engaging in ritual action—for the mystery is embodied in us. Another aspect of the visual was referred to in an offhand remark by one of my liturgy professors: We need a canon law that forbids the liturgical uglies. Celebrating is normal and natural for us humanoids; it is easier in a hospitable, beauty-ridden place. It is difficult to worship in a liturgical slum. We participate by allowing ourselves to soak up that beauty that reveals the beauty beyond and yet to come. We share in the beauty of space not by allowing it to distract from our action, but by allowing it to support our worshipful activity.

Dramatic participation. The dramatic is engaging. It teases out responses; it elicits; it calls us. Liturgy is a dramatic event, not in the sense of becoming a spectacle that manipulates and controls, squeezing out our emotions till we are drained dry, but in the sense of rehearsing and acting out the drama of salvation. Good liturgists, good leaders of prayer do not need Ph.D.s in drama, but all Christians need to attend to the great drama of the mystery; rescue from sin and dark death.

The drama of the mystery is enhanced through worthy performance of liturgical roles that have an inherent dramatic content: through proclamation of the Scriptures that stirs the soul; through gesture and movement that elevate the spirit; through that liturgical artistry that truly comes from above.

Ritual participation. In celebration we behave ritually; there are ritual words spoken, ritual gestures performed. We are called to be in tune with the world and with ourselves. Our ritual behavior in the assembly is no more inauthentic than our ritual behavior at basketball games, rock concerts, meals, lectures, clam bakes, at greetings and leave-takings. And the performance of ritual behavior patterns gives expression to the mystery.

We participate in ritual parades—processions, symbol-actions of the church assembling, not merely a functional means of moving ministers and others to their places; we share in common postures of kneeling, standing, of lifting our hands in prayer, not because some Roman rubrician has thus decreed, but because our inner life is expressed bodily. We share in the eucharistic meal by offering to one another the blessed bread broken for us, and the blessing cup poured out for us. In this ritual gesture of giving and receiving there is an eloquent unspoken commentary on the Christian life, made real in that moment.

Silent participation. "Be still and know that I am God" (Ps. 46) Scripture admonishes. The silence that is participatory, attending to the mystery, is far different from that of Simon and Garfunkel's "Sounds of Silence"—it is activity, contemplative activity, an expression of devotion. Its analog is the silence that obtains in basketball double overtime, when the spheroid is hurled at the basket as the buzzer sounds. It is attentive listening. Liturgy needs listening as much as it needs speaking. The liturgical participant should never be able to be reduced in caricature either to a mouth on a stick or a pair of ears on a broom handle. The liturgy demands a pround silence that issues forth out of amazement at the goodness of God; the silence of the heart that has been quieted and centers, that provides receptivity.

Liturgy is a "work that we do, while at the same time it is a working done in us" (Grimes, pp. 134-135). It is our playing in the presence of the God of mystery and also the playing of the God of mystery within us. What is unique in the liturgical act is not that it communicates—all ritualizations do this; what is unique is that in the liturgy we actively act in order to be acted upon (Grimes, p. 134ff.). In the liturgy we pray so that the Spirit may pray in us. The participatory event is in one sense preparatory; it opens us for receptivity. In another sense, it fills us with the Spirit of God already present.

LITURGICAL ENEMIES

I would like to conclude with an examination of what hinders and what aids participation, confining my remarks to the actual manner of participating in the eucharist. This section is more in the form of a litany, rather than protracted reflections.

Liturgical enemy number one is **ineffective planning**. Planning is ineffective, in the first case, if it is nonexistent. "Why, it's all right there in the missalette! Who has to plan?" The response is: All local communities, desiring to celebrate the liturgy, need to plan.

Planning is ineffective if it is not done in concert. The director of music choosing some tunes at home, the presiding minister preparing the homily without benefit of communal reflection, the liturgical artists and environicists (!) fabricating their crafts in isolation—all this leads to a collage approach to the liturgical act, rather than to a communal activity that possesses an inherent rhythm: an ebb and a flow that allows the community to move collectively in its communitarian relationship with God. Planning is ineffective if the rhythm of the liturgical year is bypassed. Planning needs to be long range, as well as immediate, so that the appropriation of the mystery is an adventure, filled with excitement, and not hokey-relevance of a carte-blanche quasi-liturgical happening. Planning is ineffective if it is overdone. Planning that programs every liturgical jot and every title moves toward manipulation and no room is left for the Spirit to move where the Spirit will.

Enemy number two, **lack of balance**, takes on various forms.

Confusion of ministerial roles. Creation of the liturgical superman distracts from participation. The liturgical superperson not only welcomes the assembly, proclaims the word and collects the offering, but leads the singing, presents the gifts, turns the pages of the sacramentary, and distributes communion. Lack of coordination and articulation of ministries hinders the participatory performance that is requisite; and it creates a very blurry ecclesiology.

Excessive musicality. Perhaps it seems strange to mention this liturgical aberration to musicians, many of whom belong to a church that is only now discovering the real horizon of liturgical music. Very often, however, there is an inverse proportionality between the amount of so-called active participation and reflection on the mystery itself.

Singing gives expression to our unity (and perhaps more often than desired to our diversity, as when four-part harmony suddenly picks up an extraneous fifth), heightens our sense of awareness of the great mystery. But judgment needs to be made, not only about the quality and music and poetic text, but also about the quantity. Congregational singing of four or five hymn tunes or thirty-nine verses of one hymn during the communion rite is a sufficient warrant for the ignorant to bad-mouth all the reforms of Vatican II. Lack of attention to the function of music within the liturgical context leads to poor participation. Dirge-like acclamations that require plodding before they come forth, Alleluias lacking lilt, music used as filler or insulation for the celebration—all these are errors of imbalance.

Attenuation of rites. If the primary liturgical symbol-actions are attenuated, they cannot speak of themselves. They will inspire insipid commentaries on the symbolic rites. If we cannot distinguish in the very act itself the greeting of peace from a love-in, if we cannot discern that the meal elements are bread and wine, if we cannot believe that the prayer of the faithful is the prayer of the actual community, if we cannot see the presented gifts as coming from this community and not a musty sacristy closet, if ministers are ritually separated from the praying community, then we cannot share, we cannot take ownership of this event. All this ritualization then degenerates into so much eyewash.

Brittle rigidity or incessant flux. The extremes of calcification of the shape of celebration or the opposite of a totally free-wheeling celebration inhibit participation. In neither case can the assembly express its ownership of the event. In the former, everything is programmed with an antiseptic automation that allows for no personal investment; in the latter, everything is up for grabs and the assembly is confused. If the shape constricts or if the framework is unrecognizable, there can be no genuine communitarian expression, actualizing the mystery.

As an aside, it appears to me that missalettes often become hindrances to full, conscious, active participation. Crutches necessary immediately after Vatican II to introduce the liturgical reforms, they can now prevent even the able-bodies from walking. It is good to reflect on the fact that valid worship pre-dated the missalette.

WHAT HELPS PARTICIPATION?

To conclude on a positive note, let me give another litany. What helps participation?

1. The existence of a real community, a group of Christians who are involved in one another's lives.

2. The daily appropriating of the mystery of the life and death of Jesus as the paradigm of living. This leads to sparkling eucharistic celebrations.

3. Well-prepared celebrations, prepared by the planning team with the presiding minister present at the planning session.

4. Well-trained readers, whose proclamation of the Scripture makes the words leap off the page, whose proclamation celebrates *the* Word and not merely words.

5. Excellent musicians—instrumentalists, vocalists, choirs, cantors, song leaders. Musicians who understand their pastoral role of leading and ministering to the praying community, whose ministry calls the community to pray, not to listen to their performance of music.

6. Skilled liturgical artists, who care for the environment for worship, whose crafts of drama, plastic, and spatial arts, and rhythmic arts inspire and uplift.

7. Prayerful leaders of prayer who call forth from the community *its* prayer.

In short, what helps participation is a real community of faith that recognizes the Body of Christ where it is, and then behaves accordingly.

I conclude with the words of Aidan Kavanagh: "Participation . . . is just about anything you care to make it—unless it is first of all full membership in the Church, by conversion, faith, hope and charity: one heart in love. Nothing more. But nothing less. Amen" (Kavanagh, p. 353).

References

Abhishiktanada. *Prayer.* SPCK, London, 1967.

Daniélou, Jean. "Le Symbolisme des rites baptismaux," *Dieu Vivant*, no. 1-3, 1945, pp. 17-43.

Feuillet, André. *The Apocalypse.* Translated by Thomas E. Crane. Alba House, 1964, pp. 73-74, 85-88.

Grimes, Ronald L. "Modes of Ritual Necessity." *Worship* 53 (March, 1979), 126- 141.

Kavanagh, Aidan. "What Is Participation? or Participation Revisited." *Doctrine and Life* 23 (July, 1973), 343-353.

Neunhauser, B. "Les Leçons du passé pour la participation à la messe." *Les Questions Liturgiques et Paroissiales*, 109-127.

Roguet, A.M., "Participation in the Mass: The Theological Principles," in *Pastoral Studies II*, pp. 120-137.

Nouwen, Henri. "Compassion: The Core of Spiritual Leadership." *Worship* 51 (January 1977), 11-23.

Seasoltz, R. Kevin. "Christian Prayer: Experience of the Experience of Jesus' Dying and Rising." *Worship* 53 (March, 1979) 98-119.

Seasoltz, R. Kevin. "Symbolizing Immanence and Transcendence." *Worship* 50 (September, 1976) 386-412.

Eugene Walsh

TWO

"THINGS AIN'T WHAT THEY USED TO BE"

What I want to do here is, first to uncover a basic self-deception that we work under new liturgy, which keeps us doing it wrong; second, to point the direction that will help us do it right.

Let's take self-deception. The first point is that as long as we put liturgy ahead of service in the life of the parish, we are bound to miss the main reason for the parish to exist at all. The church's main mission on earth, and therefore the main mission of any given parish, is to reach out to people with the reconciling Good News of Jesus, with the compassion of Jesus, with the service of Jesus. The mission of the church is best understood when we call a parish community a community of disciples. Disciples are necessarily outward bound. The church, says Juan Segundo, is the only organization in the whole world that does not exist primarily for the sake of its own members. As long as the people of a parish give primary attention to what they do in church and not to what they do outside of church, they are bound to become self- centered and self-serving. That is the way most parish members think of their parish: the parish exists most of all to serve its members. But that is just not so.

Worship exists, of course, to praise the Lord. But God does not need our worship. We need it. Worship feeds us, gives us renewed faith and commitment to the Gospel, new courage to get outside and do the job of Christians in the world. A parish that is concerned primarily with its mission of service outside and is committed to that mission, will necessarily work for a life-giving worship, because nothing else will nourish its members adequately.

21

The second self-deception leads equally in the wrong direction. Up to now and continuing into the "next now," it seems that most parishes engaged in the renewal of worship are focused on "doing" things differently, on "getting it right" according to the new guidelines. I see as much concern to "get it right" in the renewed church as there was in the old church about rubrics. Rubrics or guidelines or whatever, of themselves can never make a life-giving liturgy. They are just dry bones without flesh, or even look-alive flesh without life and spirit.

This criterion for celebrating Sunday Mass leaves the life-energy of sacramental celebrations untouched. That is why most parishes, without necessarily realizing it, are supporting and continuing the "custodial care and minimal maintenance" syndrome. It is like "business as usual" with a new look: more ministers, rearranged furniture, different music sounds, but not too much change in the minds and hearts of the people. But parish worship comes to life only when everybody, and I do mean everybody, every member of the assembly, understands *what* they are doing and *why* they are doing it. Vatican II has given us a new vision of church and sacraments. This vision brings with it radically new and profoundly revolutionary understandings and insights. Things are different. Things will never be the way they were again.

I want to take a fresh look at what is truly revolutionary in the new church and to say why. Then I want to point out some areas where genuine conversion is necessary if we will continue to grow into adulthood in the church.

A New Vision of Church

I think that the greatest gift of Vatican II is the restoration in our time of the full vision of the church, a vision that has been missing for a long time. During the sixth to eighth centuries, the so-called dark ages, the full vision of church got dimmed out and shriveled up. The horizontal dimension of church was quite effectively squeezed out. What came out of the squeeze was a vertical church. But that is only one part of the church. This vertical church was a clergy church. The people were effectively relegated to the position of lookers-on, of spectators. The people of the church became truly second-class citizens. The vertical church was deprived of their voice and energy. The vertical church, therefore, became deprived of that part of the voice of the Spirit that can be heard only through the voice of the people. The church became, in a very real sense, a crippled church. It was not able to work up to the full vision and possibilities of church as it was intended to be.

The lost horizontal dimension of church has been restored to us in our time. Vatican II is telling us that the church is, before all else, God's people, God's priestly people. *We* are church, all of us: clergy and people together. The church is *us*. By way of Vatican II the church has claimed again the community dimension of church. It has restored to its vertical dimension the marvelous, life-giving horizontal dimension. It is as if we get to have the whole church back together again. We have given the lie to the humpty dumpty story.

This is a wonderful vision, a vision full of wonder. All Christian people, all baptized Christians, are called back to first-class citizenship. The vertical church has finally admitted that adults in the church are really adults. Church leaders, from the pope on down, are trying to cope with this new idea, because it is new for all of us. This revolutionary turn-about will take time, but it is on the way. Church leaders will never again be able to deal with adults in the church as if they were children. Learning to do that is going to take a while.

All adults in the church are called back to full responsibility for the entire mission of the church: to celebrate liturgy, not to sit back and watch someone else do it; to make community, to make parish assembly, to change ourselves from individuals into a "people," a deliberately conscious people of God; and after that to go outside of church to proclaim the Good News where it needs to be heard, and, most of all, to serve brothers and sisters in their need, wherever they are and whomever they are.

A New Vision of Sacraments

This new mission of church accompanies a new vision of sacraments. Within the larger world the church is "the" sacrament of Jesus. The church has been chosen by the free action of God to be the body of Christ in the world, to be the sign to the world that God is in the world working to save all people and to bring them to God's kingdom of peace, freedom, and love. To the church Jesus gave his own mission in the world: to go forth and proclaim the Good News of God's saving plan and to make the kingdom come. This is why the church is, before all other sacraments, "the" sacrament of encounter with Jesus. This is why Juan Segundo says that the only difference between the church and all the rest of God's people is that the church are those "who know."

Within the church Jesus calls upon all baptized people to make the body signs that we call sacraments. Jesus calls upon all members of the assembly to reach out to each other in human care and concern. In the celebration of the sacraments Jesus calls upon his people to break down the barriers of selfishness and hatred and discrimination and all that is evil. In the celebration of sacraments Jesus depends upon his people in the church to open themselves up to each other, to give all those who are present the chance to experience his presence, to enter into union with him by entering into union with one another.

Today the church is telling us that we have a great deal to do about the life-giving quality of a sacrament. Jesus asks us to work with him in a generous cooperative way to make sacraments. Jesus charges us to take the trouble to make vigorous, living human signs. Jesus comes to us through us. He has chosen to do it that way. We have the power to open the way of Jesus to people or to cut him off. That is a big responsibility.

It is still true that there is always some life in any sacramental action no matter how poorly the sign comes off. But so is there some life in a person who is on support systems in an intensive care unit. The machines tell us that there are some vital signs. But the life-giving energy is minimal, almost negligible, compared to what we know and accept as truly alive and life-giving persons.

The church is now telling us to look at the life-giving quality of the sign itself. Life-giving signs make life-giving sacraments. You get life when you take the trouble to give life, your own life. This is precisely what the word "celebration" means. You celebrate a sacrament when you take the trouble "to share" what you think and feel about each other and about God and Jesus and people.

If you do not share yourself in the sacramental moment you do not really celebrate.

If you want to determine the life-giving quality of a given eucharist on Sunday, all you need to do is to look around. For instance, you have a large church, one-third to a half full, people scattered all over, hopelessly and helplessly isolated from one another. They are not speaking to one another; they are not paying attention to one another. They are buried in their own books, so much that they don't even look up half the time to see what is going one. So long as they read it, everything is O.K. Passivity and disconnectedness all over the place. Is the sign life-giving or not?

In such a situation there is a basic question that must be asked. How much church really exists in that building? How much eucharist really takes place? Church and eucharist do not exist in a life-giving manner apart from participation by the people. If you say they do, you are talking about magic. And magic is what the sacraments are not.

A Call to Conversion

All these revolutionary changes in the theology of church and sacrament depand a radical conversion on our part. Genuine conversion takes place only when we *see* things differently, *understand* things differently than before. Serious and lasting conversion begins with an insight. The first step for conversion is "Change your mind!" After that and only after that comes "Change your heart!" Without insight, without change of mind, what we call conversion is shallow and short-lived. The big change called for in the church today is conversion of mind and heart. And mind comes first.

This new theology demands a radical turnabout for the whole church, but particularly for all leaders in the church. We are asked to think differently and to act differently in areas that we have taken for granted through many years, areas that have been unquestioned and unquestionable. This is a big step for everyone. If we do not take the step, we will not move into the future. If parishes do not move ahead, they will continue their lackluster and self-centered task of providing custodial care and minimal maintenance for those who still bother to come.

The Exodus journey is the most important biblical image of the church we have. It tells us all about Israel and all about Jesus and all about church. The church is on a journey, a freedom march from bondage to freedom, to a freedom that we cannot make for ourselves, a freedom that God has prepared for us. Our freedom journey is rooted in the past. We can never cut ourselves off from our roots. That means death.

But rooted in the past does not mean mired in the past. All journeys are, by their very nature, future-directed. People on a journey are always moving forward, spurred on by the vision that shines ahead of them. They do remember where they have been, but they are most concerned to get on to what comes next. They are always determining what of the past has become useless and is dead weight on the journey. They dump useless baggage. That is precisely what Vatican II did. That is what our present reform is all about.

The church is by its very nature future-directed. When we dig in and insist on staying where we are because of security and nostalgia for the past, we frustrate God's will to make the king-dom come. Most of us grew up in a church that was very safe and secure. Things were always in their expected place. You could always be quite sure where you were. For instance, when you went to Mass in those days, all you had to really do was to be present some way or the other. After that what you did during Mass made little difference. You could follow what the priest was doing from a distance, or you could pray your own private pray-ers. The point was very simple. The Mass belonged to the priest. He did the whole thing and all you did was to watch him do it. That is how you got grace.

Now the church is saying that the Mass does not belong to the priest as his private possession. It belongs to the whole church. "The church makes the eucharist; the eucharist makes the church," as Yves Congar stated it. The parish assembly is the first and primary minister of Sunday Mass. But within the assembly are distinct and different ministries. The priest is chosen and empowered by ordination to preside over the eucharistic action and to lead the assembly in prayer. There are other ministers with specific tasks. When the ministers put it all together with deliberate care and concern, we get a beautiful and totally life-giving celebration.

This vision of the church, although new to us, is very traditional. It is more traditional than the view of the church and eucharist we have been used to. It is the vision of the church that created the incredible discipleship of the early church.

Life-Giving Celebrations

If we could be converted to this vision of church, great and wonderful things would happen. First, more and more members of the parish assembly would begin to realize that they have something important and indispensable to contribute to the celebration of Mass. They would begin to realize that their contribution is most essential to life-giving eucharist. Second, we would begin to realize that the full, life-giving symbol of eucharist is not bread and wine. These are only partial signs of eucharist. The full sign and symbol of the eucharist is the assembly fully aware of themselves as God's people, deliberately sharing themselves with each other through the actions of *gathering* with each other, *listening* to God's word, and *responding* through eucharistic action and through service to brothers and sisters afterwards.

When you see it this way, it becomes very clear what you are supposed to do to make the eucharist as truly life-giving sacrament. Bring the full symbol of eucharist to life, help the assembly bring itself to life. Nothing else substitutes for this sign.

So I suggest for all those who would create life-giving celebrations: Think assembly! Focus assembly! Get a single-minded preoccupation with one question: How can we help the assembly bring itself to life? How can we work with the assembly to help them produce those life-giving energies that make life: the energies of gathering and listening and responding through eucharistic action and through mission outside? Music people, for example, need to become obsessed with the first commandment for music ministers as expressed so perceptively by Charles Gardner in the April-May 1983 issue of *Pastoral Music*. Let it become the cry of the new age! "Pastoral musicians must learn the love the sound of a singing congregation above any other musical sound."

The Faith Experience

Genuine conversion demands that we take another look at that vague business we call the faith experience. We spend a lot of time and energy trying to create that faith experience, in trying to catch God and hold God present in our midst. Much of this time and energy is wasted because we really do not know what we are doing. Let's take a look.

First off, the faith experience is the experience of God in our midst. Nothing more or less. But God alone can make the faith experience happen because God is the only one who can make God-self present and available to us. God and God alone initiates any authentic faith experience and does so through Jesus in the power of the Spirit. If the experience does not come from God, then we can be sure that we are on a self-delusion trip that is emanating from our own glands.

Our contribution is twofold: first, to be open and willing for Jesus to come. Second, to reach out to one another through deliberate and attractive human signs. Through them we open the doors through which Jesus enters, the doors to the sacred. Through them we break down the barriers that keep us separated from each other and therefore from Jesus.

All of this by way of saying that the more warmly human a celebration is, the more sacred and transcendent it can become. Once we have seen it this way and have accepted this very clear and wonderful fact, we stop playing tricks with lights and soft music and medieval garb and incense in order to get what I call "pretend" transcendence. I am not against the proper use of any of these signs when they are used in light of the principles we are talking about. Someday, however, I am going to experience a reconciliation rite that does not call for a seeing eye dog to get around and that winds up in a blaze of light and sound and excitement, because that is what God's mercy and forgiveness are all about.

Active Participation

For a long time I thought I knew what active participation was all about. Then, all of a sudden, I realized that I really did not understand it at all. I had it backwards, so that what I thought was active participation was really passive participation, if we can use that term. I discovered with help that most of the things we do in our efforts to encourage active participation are really reinforcing the passivity of the assembly.

Up to now we have taken participation to mean lively response to something that other people have already prepared for you. It has been very much like eating a meal that someone else has prepared. You are quite active in consuming it, but you had nothing to do with making it in the first place. Genuine, active participation means that the people know that they have an active and important part in making the Mass celebration happen, and set about the task of doing their part in making it happen. It is the difference between making it happen and "having some" of what someone else has made.

Full, deliberate, active, conscious participation of all the people in the celebration of Mass is the stated goal of all liturgical reform and renewal. When members of the assembly take personal responsibility for gathering and being hospitable at Mass, you begin to have active participation. When people take full responsibility to connect themselves with the proclaimed word by serious listening, you have deliberate and conscious active participation, as also when they take the trouble to involve themselves in the eucharistic action and in the mission of the church outside.

"Up with Signs! Down with Words!"

This should also become the rallying cry of our conversion. There is little evidence that we really believe in signs, which is very close to saying that there is not much evidence that we really believe in sacraments, the way they ought to be believed in. We do not trust signs to stand by themselves. We put a crown on a man, wrap an ermine robe about his body, put a chain of gold around his neck, and a scepter in his hand. We take a look, shake our heads, and go look for a sign that says: This is the king. And we hang it around his neck just to be sure.

There is overwhelming evidence that we believe in words and words and words. Verbal overkill shoots the sign to death and leaves the corpse lying in a mess all over the church floor. Just take a look on Sunday at the glazed eyeballs, at the almost frantic effort not to pay attention. See the powerful dedication of people to reading every blessed word of the whole thing, and in their own private book. Note the utter anonyance when someone departs one syllable from the script. These people are involved in words only. They are not involved in the eucharistic sign. They are not doing anything to bring the sign of life. They are unable to do anything to help give life to the sign because they are paralyzed with word. Involvement in words cuts them off from the sign as effectively as the rood screen used to do in the medieval cathedral.

When you have nothing better to do, count all the words we use in one celebration of the eucharist: before Mass, at the beginning of Mass, during the penitential rite, dull recitation of prayers, meaningless introductions to the scripture readings, long and extended petitions of the prayer of the faithful, not to mention the short and brilliant homily. The signs don't have a chance. They are drowned in words. Often musicians are just as guilty. How much you talk in trying to get people to sing! You could sing it five times during the time you take to explain. Here again a dramatic conversion is called for. "Up with signs! Down with words!" No greater gift can you give to a captive, weary, and oppressed assembly.

We are not finished yet. There is more to come. We need a complete turn-about in how we think of the Mass as prayer. The Mass is not a private devotional prayer done by individuals who are gathered into the same room at the same time. The celebration of Mass is a *public prayer, a public action* done by a *people* who make it happen by working together deliberately. This is what it is supposed to be, but this is not what it is in practice.

For the most part, all of us come to church as individuals. We remain individuals while we are there. Holy communion is the high point of Mass for most people. And holy communion is thought to be intensely private. Hardly anyone sees it as a public act of a people. We go home as individuals. This is the way we have been brought up. It is entirely understandable. But it has to change if we would make the Mass become the life-giving energy it is supposed to be.

In more recent years Catholic people have been hearing a great deal about their being God's people, made so by baptism. But they have not come to the point of realizing what this means and the responsibilities that go with it. The reason is that they have heard it in words, but have not had much chance to experience it. "The church makes the eucharist; the eucharist makes the church." People begin to experience themselves as church, as God's people, only when they begin to act as a church. We act as a church when we work together through gathering, listening, responding to make the eucharist happen in a life-giving way. When we work to make the eucharist happen, we are at the same time being formed into church through the experiences we are sharing. It is just like family. We learn that we are a family only by living it out. We don't get too many lectures on it. So it is with learning that we are God's people. We have to live it out together while we are hearing about it.

All this means that we who are leaders have a big job to do. We have got to help people understand why and what and how they celebrate. And, like all learning this understanding happens when people experience good celebrations and are given the time to reflect together on what they experience. We have no excuse. We have got to find a way. Some people *have* found the way to go, and it *can* work!

Celebrating
with a Community
of Children

THREE

"BLESSED BE JESUS WHOM YOU SENT TO BE THE FRIEND OF CHILDREN"

When the Directory for Masses with Children, issued by the Sacred Congregation for Divine Worship, was first published in 1973, it was hailed by many as opening a new chapter in the development of liturgies celebrated by and with children. It took some time, but this assessment has proven to be true. However, the Directory is not just a manual containing principles, suggestions, and options; it is also a document which challenges us to live a new vision of what we are called to be as church. In this article I would like to highlight seven visionary principles contained in the first chapter of the Directory and, by way of conclusion, I will then briefly list a few references to some creative solutions.

SEVEN PRINCIPLES

First Principle

The first principle is that a fully Christian life requires living the paschal mystery through participation in liturgy as an assembly. There are three elements to this principle: (1) participation in the liturgy; (2) assembly; (3) the paschal mystery.

First, participation. Vatican II's famous directive about full, conscious, active participation in the liturgy has been terribly misunderstood, and the misconceptions are being handed down to our children.

The historical context for the notion of full, active, conscious participation began in the late 1880s with the development of Communist-Marxist philosophy, which said that bourgeois society excluded the common person from participation, and that it was very important for people to throw off the upper class and begin to participate in the development of society. The Roman Catholic Church, totally committed to a principle of communitarianism, emphasized that it too believed in the importance of full participation and encouraged persons to participate in social reforms, the social aspects of its life, caring for one another, and the like. And it indicated that participation would reflect from activity in the society into full, active, conscious participation in the eucharistic celebration at Sunday liturgy. This act of full, conscious participation would be transformative of the whole person.

In 1963, when the Vatican Council occurred, our society was in the midst of a tremendous social revolution of active involvement. And so, full conscious participation became the active ingredient, the banner call-word for a social revolution that swept through the American church. Then people quite literally picked up the folk guitar and began singing a new repertoire in church. The texts of the songs were not freedom-protest texts, but certainly the melodic forms and the social cultural forms were part of this movement.

People got the idea that a sing-along liturgy was the goal of full, conscious, active participation. They thought, from their experience, that full, conscious, active participation meant getting the people to sing, at any cost, any song. But active participation for children and for adults is not singing along at Mass— whether it be good music or bad, folk or traditional— but the transformative action of one's life through ritual.

Second, assembly. Assembly has come to mean the actual church at worship, the parish community gathered in the act of worship. Perhaps the most daring insight that has come from the vision of assembly is that all members are before all else equal— readers, musicians, hospitality ministers, ushers, members of the assembly, and, especially, presider are all first members of the assembly because of the priesthood of baptism. We gather as disciples of Jesus.

Third, paschal mystery. Paschal mystery can be religious jargon—God-talk that puts off both parents and children. So we need to decode the term: *paschal* means passover or Easter, or the passing of Jesus from death to life. *Mystery* is a technical term here meaning sacrament or sign of that which is yet to be revealed. Paschal mystery is the act of passing from death to life, the transformation of Jesus—his full, active participation in the will of his Father made present to us through signs. It provides us with the hope that when we die, we will pass to life.

Not all children's liturgy is eucharistic, but it should all be implicitly paschal. And this is true as well for the whole people of God. I'm not talking about the language but about the depth of vision. Anyone who lacks such a depth of vision ought not to presume to exercise liturgical ministry for anyone, especially children. What are the signs of the paschal mystery within us? How do we see the transformation taking place within us? The metaphor of being a child is in fact moving out of that state we call childhood into adulthood. It is a paschal mystery. Our growth, our life is a paschal mystery. We imitate the master by moving away from our childhood to our adulthood.

This leads us to an important principle for pastoral practitioners: childhood is a state unto itself and it is of its very nature a transition to another state. Part of our effort to help the child is made by adapting to the state that exists, and part of our effort must be to call the child to a new stage of development. Support and confrontation cannot exist simultaneously. Too much or too little of either will destroy the child's personality.

Second Principle

The second principle is that all who have a part in the formation of children should consult and work together. This is obvious. But the Sacred Congregation on Worship goes further: its says *why* we should work together. All should work together so that the children can experience the human values first. What are the human values that the Congregation means? We are told we should all work together:

1. so that the human value of community activity can be experienced by the child—the human value of gathering, sharing, talking, socializing;

2. that the child should experience the exchange of greetings, salutations, and embraces—that very human act of saying "The Lord be with you," "peace be with you"—as an act and manifestation of the church;

3. that children have the capacity to listen, that they should be in the presence of the Scriptures proclaimed, not because they're going to understand them but because they can witness the adults experiencing a listening;

4. that they have a capacity to see and gain pardon: the Congregation says that "children should witness this act of adults forgiving and being forgiven"—this human exchange of asking for and being forgiven—as a human action, not as some power from on high;

5. that the children should feel an expression of gratitude . . . that somehow, in the assembly, the feeling of thanks and sharing should be so intense that the children can witness it;

6. that they can experience the meal as a meal of friendship; that children can recognize the eucharist as a meal would be vision enough, but it must also be clear that these are friends gathered, loving one another;

7. and that they can share in the festive celebration, the trumpets and the banners and the dancers and the song: if the children can witness this, then they will naturally participate—their responses may disturb our adult sense of order, but they have much to teach us.

The Congregation says: Teach the human values first, and the "children will gradually open their minds to the perception of the Christian values and the celebration of the mystery of Christ" (no. 9). In church we are not the parents of our children. They are the children of the community. Anyone can take charge of them.

If we are going to educate our children along these lines, then we are going to have to reform our parishes. The presumption of this document is the same that many have learned from the document on the rite for Christian initiation of adults: our parishes are presumed to be human communities, communities that are shared. The Congregation is saying that our assemblies on

Sunday must reflect these strong human values if our children are to be formed. What is envisioned here is a dramatic overhaul of Christian parishes, and it begins with the human, the ordinary, the everyday.

Third Principle

The third principle is that the Christian family has the greatest role in teaching these human values. Gabe Huck's *Family at Prayer* teaches how the Christian family is a house church, the first Christian assembly, and how the seasons of the year must be made visible in that church; all the rhythms of the child's life— not just the school year, summer vacation, going to school, watching television—but something of the rhythm of the natural cycle of our lives, the death, the birth of our seasons, our time, the sanctification of our cycles. And music must be experienced in the family. Music is too important to the cultural development of the human race to be denied to and omitted from the experience of our children; and not just music-*listening* but music-*making*. Even the nonsingers and nonmusicians need to participate in these basic human sounds. Music is part of everyday living, not just an exotic fare for sophisticates.

Fourth Principle

The fourth principle is that the Christian assembly has a responsibility for the children in three ways: to give witness to the Gospel; to live with fraternal charity; and to actively celebrate the mysteries of Christ.

What a vision the Directory has! The Christian community in the formation of itself is measured by its ability to proclaim the Gospel and to be bonded one to the other.

The community must attend to its exceptional children. A real problem is that adults tend to deny the child in themselves. We learn to hide, to mask as we grow older, and the child has a great, built-in manure detector. When you work with children, you can't hide behind partial or masked things; they'll expose you. It's really remarkable—when you sing bad music, the children get embarrassed first. They know it before the adults.

The community has the responsibility of serving both the beginning musician and the most advanced child. Genius in children is recognized in math and music. We must provide a place within the Roman Catholic institution where children gifted in music can begin to be identified and recognized.

Fifth Principle

Catechetical programs should be directed toward the Mass. While the bishops' instruction to us lists four elements that should be emphasized— namely, the children's participation, the relation of the Mass to the world, the eucharistic prayer, and the acclamations—I'd like to direct our attention to the last of these, the acclamations during the eucharistic prayer. Music plays a unique role in the acclamations.

The three acclamations we are concerned with here are the Holy, Holy, the Memorial, and the Great Amen. If we are to judge from the way they are sung in most liturgies, the importance of these acclamations needs to be taught not only to the children, but to everyone. We must learn that, through the Holy, the assembly joins all creation past and present and places itself in the presence of the one, eternal worship of God. We must learn that singing the Memorial is doing the memorial, the most solemn command of our master. And we must learn that Amen is the most important prayer the Christian utters. It is a covenant with God as life-giver. It binds us to live as brothers and sisters with all people on earth.

Sixth Principle

The Congregation advises us to use celebrations, but avoid giving them a didactic purpose.

Is the purpose of liturgy to celebrate or educate? When it is celebrative, it is the symbolic actions that are central. Liturgy understood as celebration is at the heart of the formation process. Liturgy, which properly speaks to the heart more than the head, forms us through experience. Education, which speaks to the head more than to the heart, engages us in reflection on our experiences. Both are essential. The biggest error that we could make is to isolate children into some sort of religious education class and to provide adults with only didactic worship.

Emphasis on children's participation in celebrative liturgy, and Christian formation through liturgy, can make some adults uncomfortable. Those who see religion as only rational are dismayed. Liturgy that shapes our character and perceptions through art, poetry, drama, dance and music; through sight, touch, taste, sound and smell, through the repetition of symbolic words and actions, is scary to some. Didactic liturgy is not the appropriate place for children. Boring liturgy is not the proper place for children or for adults.

We know that the child's imagination should be developed. It is this knowledge that causes many parents to move away from boredom that exists in the Sunday liturgy and toward a ministry with children. But, as a result of television, the entertainment mentality of the child and, unfortunately, of the parent who is involved, we often combat this boredom with a ministerial approach that leads to doing children's liturgies based on "Sesame Street," ninety-second concentration spans, or the "Brady Bunch." The goal of entertainment is a false one for liturgy.

Ritual rooted in truly human gathering, forgiving, sharing, greeting, and festivity will engage the child. This is the routine profundity of ritual.

Seventh Principle

Everything should be aimed at the response in the life of the child. It is the child who must put his or her religious experience into practice, not simply by celebrating, but by living out the Christian life.

Religious experience and the arts are related. So are religious experience and the liturgy. The distance that we have put between ourselves and the arts and the church has impoverished our religious experience and diminished the effectiveness of our liturgies. Technological Christianity with its concern for the intellect, and enlightenment Christianity with its concern for morality have sometimes been insensitive to experience and the affections. Witness the design element in most Catholic churches. We cannot make sense of that which we have not experienced. We have forgotten that the formation of character is prior to the education of conscience. Orthodoxy has overshadowed orthopraxis. We must be careful, therefore, that our cultic life is not dominated by the discursive, the rationalistic, the didactic, and the prosaic.

Good ritual focuses primarily on the role of the symbolic. This is not to defend a shallow asceticism or emotionalism but to suggest that our rituals are often characterized by too much discussion, stereotyped actions, mundane music, unimaginative drama, nonexistent dance, and naturalistic art. When worship is dominated by the art and is celebrative, children are at home and can fully paticipate. They are nurtured and formed as Christians.

We give our children the most nourishing food. Why would we want to give them dried up sounds? They deserve not our least music, but our best music.

CREATIVE SOLUTIONS

I have laid out a vision from the Directory for Masses with Children. Contained in this vision is a hope that parish worship can be better, that what is needed is a reform, not only of ourselves, but of the parish communities where we find ourselves, so that what the next generation will find is warm, loving, human communities. We need to:

1. be human;

2. keep the parents from entertainment-only liturgy;

3. develop *music* education programs in the parish, even if they are in the school;

4. develop children's choirs;

5. attend to the gifted musical child;

6. help the "non-singer" teacher in religious education.

It's going to take creative solutions. It's not going to be easy. Music educators have been involved in this for years and years, and music educators have been struggling with these problems again and again. But if we work in a slow, methodical, nonexaggerated, non-instant-transformational way, then we can indeed build a place where our children can find the values we all believe in. This is the vision, a vision we are to become.

FOUR

LITURGY WITH CHILDREN: BASIC LITURGICAL PRINCIPLES

The Introduction to the Directory for Masses with Children begins:

> The church shows special concern for baptized children who have yet to be fully initiated through the sacraments of confirmation and eucharist as well as for children who have only recently been admitted to holy communion. (no. 1)

At first glance this is not a very astonishing sentence. It seems merely to establish the age range for the children whom this document has in mind, that is, those who have not yet been confirmed. But the phrasing reminds us of something the church has lately had very much on its mind, Christian initiation. Membership in the church is not the finished result of a single, simple decision or ritual, but is rather the gathering reality of a process that may take a number of years. The Rite of Christian Initiation of Adults (RCIA) has revolutionized the way in which adults are welcomed into Catholicism, reflecting the shift from a static to a dynamic understanding of membership in the church. Thus the opening sentence of the Directory for Masses with Children should be understood to say that issues concerning Masses with children must be addressed within the context of the initiation process our children are going through.

The Directory is unique, the only document of the Roman Church concerned particularly with children as children. The section on "children of catechetical age" in the RCIA, for example, is an adaptation, a deviation from the norm. Likewise, the Rite of Penance, though used appropriately with children, is designed for the adult as norm and model. The Directory, therefore, is the only charter we have for our work with children. It is important, then, to understand what is underneath it and not just its specific directives and suggestions.

INITIATION OF CHILDREN

Christian initiation is a process. It requires time. It requires living. Liturgy has an important, creative role to play in marking that process, clarifying it, drawing the children into it ever more deeply. We do not eat the same meal twice; neither do we come to the table twice as the same person. Nourishing our growing selves is a continuing, evolving experience. This is true both at our dinner table and at our eucharistic table. Each eucharistic celebration therefore is unique, yet each is also part of a continuum. The customs and manner of our celebration will add up for good or for ill. To paraphrase Marshall McLuhan, "prayer is a process, not a product." Like music on the page, the prescribed rituals of our prayer are only a possibility, a direction. But when sung, played, performed, the music lives. Likewise, we hold up the gospel book and say, "This is the word of the Lord," referring not to the printed page, but to the word as proclaimed, as living and grace-filled in the hearts of our listeners. This is the reality we invite our children to be part of—the living word, the living sacrament, the living liturgy of our people.

Tertullian wrote that "one is not Christian by birth, but one becomes Christian through grace and personal confession of faith." Our children, baptized though they are, still need a process of initiation into the faith they have received. As they come to know personally the God of Jesus, present and active in the love and worship of the community, they will become more capable of making their own that baptismal faith. This is not to say that the faith of this "in between" time is not real, or is less valuable because it is "only" a participation in that of parents and community. It is very real, very valuable. It is simply the faith that is characteristic of children.

The RCIA is the key expression of the church's concern with the process of initiation. What instruction does it offer for dealing with persons who are in this process? First, it describes initiation into a Christian community as a journey, a process, a growth. While it is never finished, its beginning does have a kind of rhythm to it. There are definable stages, with liturgical ceremonies to mark its moments of transition. The Directory invites us to do the same for our child-initiates.

Second, the RCIA tells those being initiated that they may expect—may demand—of the Christian community a supportive, welcoming assembly. Sponsors in particular introduce newcomers to the teaching, mores, and values of the community but in a broader sense the whole community is the bearer of the tradition. The Directory says that children too should experience a welcoming assembly. For example, the words of the homily should in some way address children, if there are a number of them present. The document goes on to say, however, that if there are adults present, they must not be left out either. In other words, children's liturgy is never to be a "kids' show," but open to the participation of all present. Thus the RCIA and the Directory say the same thing: the eucharist is an action of the entire community, and as a welcoming community we must know who is present and we must speak to all of them.

Third, the RCIA emphasizes Christianity as a model of living. We need this reminder because the Catholic community can sometimes overstress the doctrinal aspect of faith. The Directory states that "all liturgical and eucharistic formation should be directed toward a greater and greater response to the gospel in the daily life of the children" (no. 15). In the way we prepare and in the way we celebrate, whether at the eucharist or a simple classroom prayer, or blessing of the food at our dinner table, we show clearly that we are not just saying holy words and making holy gestures, but are doing something that is an integral part of a holy life. If we do not learn that message from our youngest days, we will find it very difficult to really understand or to live the Gospel.

Last, the RCIA envisions faith as a conscious, personal reality. Therefore, the leadership offered by the church to the initiate, whether adult or child, must be conscious and personal. We must know them by name. We must call them by name. We must speak their language as we share with them the legends, the lore, and the loves of our community.

This correlation between the RCIA and the Directory is a pastoral, and not a literal one. In other words, we must remember that the children we are speaking of are not catechumens. The baptism they received is fully operative, not just a pledge of things yet to come. They already live in faith. Yet, like catechumens, they are in an initiatory process that must be taken seriously. In fact, the most important message of the Directory is just this: yes, the church does take children seriously.

The story of Jesus blessing the children is instructive in this context. It is one of those few included in all three synoptic Gospels. It describes a group of parents trying to gain access to Jesus for their children. Jesus decided the issue over the objections of his "handlers," and the children came to him. According to Oscar Cullman and others, the real issue in the early church that the story points to was the children's access through baptism to the kingdom of heaven, present to the world in the person of Jesus. The phrase used by Jesus, "Do not hinder them," echoes an early baptismal formula; it is used in three baptismal scenes in Acts. It served the same purpose as the formula used at weddings: If you know why these two should not be joined, speak now or forever hold your peace; otherwise, "do not hinder them" from taking this sacramental step. The Gospel tells us, then, that the early church had some misgivings about the baptism of young children. Shall they be hindered or received? Shall they have access to the kingdom? Shall they have membership in the community?

Jesus decided the issue, but he did not end the argument. Beneath the question of baptism is the deeper question of children's ability to lead a spiritual life. Are they capable of spiritual growth? Surely they learn about God, though on a simple level, but can they experience a genuine relationship with God? In the gospel story Jesus draws the children to himself with the explanation, "of such is the kingdom of heaven." That is, children are precisely the kind of people the kingdom is all about. We have a lot to learn about the full meaning of such a statement, but at least it helps us to think through the issues surrounding children's initiation into the community.

Yes, children do have a spiritual life, if a dependent one. Having brought them into the *ecclesia* through baptism, we must not then ignore or sideline them. The parents in our community, like those of the early generations, still bring their children forward, trying to awaken the church to their children's needs. Unfortunately, the church sometimes needs a bit of prodding before it becomes responsive. All who work with children stand with and strengthen parents in this task.

MISSION TO CHILDREN

The Directory reminds us, "The Second Vatican Council had spoken in the Constitution on the Liturgy about the need of liturgical adaptation for various groups" (no. 3). When we look back at the Constitution on the Sacred Liturgy to see what was meant by "adaptation for various groups," we find that it was part of a discussion of the essential missionary posture of the church. The Council Fathers were saying that no final expression of the Gospel of Jesus Christ is suitable for all times, all places, and all peoples. The forms and formulas that have fruitfully expressed the faith have changed and developed over many centuries. They must always change when necessary, in order to serve the faith that gives rise to them in the first place. Thus the Directory directs the missionary commitment of the church toward its own children.

This should relieve the anxieties about doing children's liturgy this way or that way or the way it has "always been done." Do we dare drop one of the lectionary readings? Yes! Drop one reading. Drop two readings, perhaps, if there is a reason to do so. If we were going to Alaska to do pastoral work among the Inuit Indians, we would expect to change many of our accustomed ways of doing things. That missionary attitude whould be the mindset with which we musicians, pastors, bishops, directors of religious education, principals, liturgists, and parents approach our ministry to children. Maria Montessori did a wonderful thing when she named her schools Casa dei Bambini, Children's House. It reminded adults that they were approaching the place that properly belonged to the children; it was the adult who was the visitor, the respectful guest, and not the other way around.

If children cannot always understand everything they experience with adults in daily life, it certainly cannot be expected that everything in the liturgy will be clear to them. "Nonetheless," continues the Directory, "we may fear spiritual harm if over the years children repeatedly experience in the church things that are scarcely comprehensible to them" (no. 2). This is a sentence to memorize. "We may fear spiritual harm . . . " It is not just a little boredom, or unused potential that is at stake. We risk actual damage if over the years our children repeatedly, Sunday after Sunday, experience things in the church that are "scarcely comprehensible" to them. Adaptations, special liturgies for children, whatever the form it may take in your parish, is not an option, but an obligation.

PRINCIPLES OF ADAPTATION

The Directory lists several general principles of adaptation, and many specific suggestions. It is well to note which are which as you study the document, so that you do not feel obligated to copy all the suggestions in a slavish way. Many feel, for example, that the only way to be faithful to the document is to develop a separate liturgy of the word for children attending the parish Sunday eucharist. The Directory does strongly suggest it, and it is a popular form of liturgy in certain parts of Europe, and it has been highly successful in many parishes in the United States. Most planners in this country, however, find the idea of separating the children from the adults disturbing. They prefer to work out some other system of addressing the worship needs of the children of the community. There may not be any one suitable, appropriate, popular solution to this issue in the American church. What is needed is much more experimentation and thoughtful research. We must do our homework, know what we are about, and then go ahead and take some risks.

The Directory reminds us that the adaptations we make should not be a matter of "creating some entirely special rite but rather of retaining, shortening, or omitting some elements or of making a better selection of texts" (no. 3). These, then, are the modes of adaptation: *retaining* (certainly we do not want to re-invent the wheel for every celebration), *shortening* (not elongating!), *omitting*(yes, we can actually have a eucharistic liturgy without a penitential rite. Go through the entire Directory and list the ritual elements that are absolutely essential at every eucharistic celebration. You will find it very skeletal.), or *making a better selection of texts*.

1. *Make it concrete.* Children are by definition those who cannot reason abstractly. We don't always realize the implications this holds for children's prayer. Adults tend to announce liturgical celebrations in terms of theological themes rather than the concrete symbols and experiences of life. It is those concrete expressions that carry emotion and meaning for children—for all those who celebrate.

The psychologist Erik Erikson identifies certain powers that children have to develop during their formative years. These are a sense of trust, autonomy, initiative, and industry. Each of these depends on the other, and each can be subverted by an opposing attitude of mistrust, shame, doubt, or guilt. When children struggle with these issues during the week but find that the church has nothing to say about them on Sunday, or worse, seems to dismiss them as childish and inconsequential, then it may seem that God is saying, "I don't trust you, I don't want you to become autonomous, I don't want your initiative but only your obedience. I don't want your industry, just sit and listen because adults have all the wisdom, they know what is what!"

2. *Keep it simple.* When preparing a children's liturgy, do not add an element until you have subtracted at least one. You may not always want to celebrate a eucharistic liturgy. Simplification means that we try to *clarify* the ceremony. We clarify an algebra problem by doing it more slowly. We clarify butter by removing all the extraneous matter so that it is transparent. Simplifying the liturgy is more like clarifying butter.

3. *Attend carefully to the symbols.* The image or symbol system upon which an individual lives for the rest of his or her life develops in early childhood. This means that we carefully weigh the images and the stories that we present. We do a thoughtful job of preparation. We are not careless of the music, nor of the art, nor of the homily. There are good expressions of ritual and there are bad expressions of ritual. It takes a lifetime of study and

prayer to prepare liturgy well. We do not take it for granted. On the other hand, we cannot wait to make adaptations until we are fully educated in this field. We must get on with the task, and learn in the doing, keeping ourselves honest all the while by asking, "How much have I really put into my own education?" (Another important question: "How much is the parish putting into the education of all those people who prepare liturgies for children?")

4. *Remember that you are concerned with the paschal mystery.* All liturgy is a celebration of our dying and rising with Christ. Thus all catechesis and all other forms of Christian prayer are directed toward the Mass.

5. *The family has the key role in the initiation of children.* As the *ecclesia*, we support but do not usurp this nurturing role.

6. *Our liturgies must be a form of celebration, not education.* We all know what this means, but need reminding of it from time to time.

PRACTICAL SUGGESTIONS

The Directory offers specific practical suggestions for implementing the general principles. For Masses where the children are not the entire congregation, such as a weekend parish Mass, the document recommends what could be called the "withdrawal and return" model. The Directory is not concerned with the babysitting service for infants that fits this model, but the meeting of young children (perhaps K through 4) with adults who guide them through a liturgy of the word designed to suit their level of understanding and experience. They return to the community before the liturgy of the eucharist begins. As mentioned above, the American church has not rushed to embrace this format, but where it has been planned with creativity and energy, it has generally been very enthusiastically received.

The second model is useful when the congregation is almost entirely children, such as a school Mass. For this format the Directory offers a myriad of concrete suggestions, each of which could be the subject of a separate article. The important thing to remember is that each part of the liturgy be treated with respect.

We are not trying to create a "separate rite" for children, and so do not eliminate the same elements each time. Neither do we eliminate or add anything without knowing why we do so and what the function and dynamic of that element is in the Roman Rite. Our liturgy is not just any combination of nice prayers strung together, but the organic result of the prayer and love and expertise and anxiety and suffering and joy and hope of our people for two thousand years.

Finally, the Directory offers practical information in the way of cautions, such as the list of liturgical elements that may never be omitted from the Mass.

That is really all the guidance you need, probably more than you need to put the Directory for Masses with Children to work in your parish. However, I would like to add one bit of advice of my own: make out a five-year plan and a one-year plan. I write this for your own mental health. Dream, brainstorm, talk to others, and then sketch out the way you would like to be worshiping. That is your five-year plan. If you try to do everything in a year, you risk burning out in a matter of months. Then take your five-year plan apart and ask, "How can we take this step by step to arrive at that place, and where shall we begin?" This will be your one-year plan. This will give you perspective in moments of frustration. It will help you see beyond today's obstacles, and you will be more likely to keep at it through the long haul.

There is much good news in the church today, with regard to children. It is that the Holy Spirit is moving among them, and their baptismal faith is alive and responsive. They are nourishing our faith while we are in the midst of nourishing theirs. And that is something to celebrate.

FIVE

CHOOSE TIME AND PLACE, MINISTERS— ALL FOR CHILDREN

Planning eucharistic or paraliturgies for children can be the most exhilarating and creative opportunity of our work—second only to actually celebrating with children. Perhaps the secret of our worship, even adult worship, lies in the innocence of children. And "planning to abandon" may be the secret of all art, all liturgy.

BEFORE BEGINNING

But how can we reach a level of planning that is so effective that our children can truly worship with abandon? Three elements must be in place before the planning sessions itself: a catechetical team ministry, the support of the community, and the appropriate response.

A Catechetical Team Ministry

Just as we have struggled to develop liturgy teams in our parishes, so a catechetical team ministry should develop among celebrant, catechist, and musician.

The celebrant's role in the team is key, as are his presence to and knowledge of the children. "It is the responsibility of the priest who celebrates with children to make the celebration fes-tive, fraternal, meditative" (no. 23). Beyond that, if we can expect more, he should have simplicity and clarity in his words and gestures, spontaneity, and a spirit of abandon to match the chil-dren's natural freedom of response.

The catechist (which includes religious educators and paro-chial school teachers) offers an intimate knowledge of the chil-dren that only hours of being together can foster. Moreover, catechists have the best understanding of the children's devel-opmental stages and catechetical experiences. The catechist will provide priceless insight for the team's "pastoral judgment."

The musician brings not only a knowledge of musical resour-ces but also, what is more important, a sense of art that is too often lacking in children's liturgies. The musician's sense of par-ish liturgy and musical development complements and enhances the catechetical experience.

The talents of the celebrant, catechist, and musician (though not exclusive), when combined, can lead to effective dialogue and the basis for mutually respectful judgments and well-balanced creative worship experiences.

The Community

The true challenge of planning children's liturgies is in allow-ing them to flow from the community of children while main-aining, at the same time, the vision that these liturgies for chil-dren lead to the adult worship experience, as discussed in no. 21 of the Directory. The attempt to achieve this balance is the source of most planning dilemmas, including the musical ones.

Two conflicting tendencies co-exist. The first is to make the children's worship experience too personal and too isolated. The argument often is: "But this is how we worship in the classroom," suggesting that the liturgy is a mere continuation of the catechet-ical experience. The inherent danger is that of not viewing liturgy as a growth process that results in the ever-deepening faith re-sponse of the child in the wider parish community. The opposite tendency is to plan a children's liturgy as a watered-down ver-sion of the adult Sunday experience. For children to really experience the rites, they must explore them in unique ways. This is where creative energies must be unleashed; this is the time to explore and re-explore. No longer are we bound by the formalities and anxieties of the adult world. Here is our chance to re-experience our childhood simplicity. In creatively exploring the rites, "experiential catechesis" occurs subconsciously. It will be unnecessary, for example, to say: "The rite of peace symbolizes . . . " once the children have experienced a paraliturgy of eucharistic celebration on friendship and love. The worship experience itself offers an enriched understanding of the meaning of the rite and enables the child to bring this appreciation to future worship experiences.

A balance between these two tendencies can eventually derive from the systems of checks and balance that will evolve in the catechetical teams. By combining the talents and fortes of each team member, a natural dialogue can emerge that will have the effect of blending the extremes.

Resources

No team can work effectively to address a community without a working knowledge of the resources available, many of which can be found at one's local Catholic bookstore or diocesan liturgy or religious education office. Presumed are a knowledge of the liturgical and musical supplements for the catechetical series used, and a knowledge of the musical resources that are available for children.

THE PLANNING SESSION

The planning session itself should include three main agenda items: the celebration, the ministries, and the music.

The celebration. As emphasized in no. 27 of the Directory, well-planned periodic celebrations are more effective than frequent or daily Masses. Also more effective are smaller groups to accomodate the drastic developmental differences between different age groups: the size of the group is determined by the stage of reli-

The ministries. A sense of the diverse ministries that exist in the Christian community (no. 24) should be instilled from the earliest age. The child's active participation in all roles is important for the development of the sense of community spirit and internal preparation for celebration (no. 22). For this reason, all class members should be involved whenever possible. Guide sheets or planning aids can facilitate the distribution of duties and can serve as a checklist for details. However, if these risk becoming "fill-in- the-blank" processes, they should be discarded, lest the sense of celebration be destroyed. In addition, the children's observance of the celebrant and the "witness" of the adult participants are vital to their understanding of the community (nos. 23 and 24).

The music. The dilemma of choosing music for children's liturgies resides in balancing that addressed to the specific community (of children) with that addressed to the larger Christian community. Of course, music should be based on the classroom experience; however, music must also be chosen with the present and future parish communities in mind.

Too readily we lose sight of our role as teachers. In planning liturgies for children, we often use childish music for its "momentary high," rather than music that is truly artful and prepares the child for the adult worship experience. This is not merely an argument against trite music; appropriate repertoire is our responsibility. Yet, keep in mind that usually the untrained musician has had limited experiences, particularly in liturgical music. We have lost sight of our role as liturgical and musical teachers both of our children *and* of the entire community.

A call to higher quality music, however, requires an understanding of the present level. Songs used in the classroom may be appropriate for use at some services. The musical judgment here should be based on the development level of the child; the pastoral judgment is based on a selection's validity as a worship experience. Once again, a natural balance can emerge from dialogue between the musician and catechist. A musical understanding for the catechist and a catechetical understanding for the musician will be the basis for sound, artful worship for our children.

PREPARATION AND ABANDON

Two elements remain after the planning sessions: preparation and abandon.

Preparation. Careful, detailed preparation before the celebration cannot be stressed enough. The creativity of the celebration demands extra preparation and coordination, and children's restlessness leaves little room for last-minute details. Encouragement and development of the children's sense of ministries, and of their active participation will help engender a spirit of true community (no. 29).

Abandon! As the relationship of liturgy and catechesis deepens and matures (National Catechetical Directory, no. 113), the worship experience becomes vital to all involved with children. An amazing thing happens when we worship with children—we learn. For all present, including the presider, the catechist, the musician, and the adult worshiper, the wisdom of the children teaches us how to truly abandon ourselves to celebrate.

SIX

FATHER, KNOW YOUR CHILDREN

As the reformed liturgy took shape in the late sixties, children's liturgies often included a popular refrain: "Here we are, all together as we sing our song, joyfully." If one could read hearts, one would have seen that the joyful mood was more hope than reality.

In particular, priests were singing different refrains. Some were upset about freedom in liturgical laws. Others considered it a badge of honor to bypass the Roman Rite—as long as the bishop didn't know. Still others had to stretch their tolerance to smile through forty art works explained by their nervous creators or the zealous education director. Pastors began to draw lines about adaptation. Their education had posited various items as essential. There were no changes allowed on wearing a stole, on saying the consecration, or on having an altar stone. Anything else that was written or done by the children and their teachers was all right. There was one pastor who allowed anything at outdoor Masses as long as he was given an oriental rug behind the altar, a white altar cloth, and candles shielded from the wind.

Some might like to believe otherwise, but it seems that the same confusion and fear lives in many parishes. The role of the clergy at children's liturgies is still in need of clarification. The answer does not lie in a new or old legalism. We do not need priests whose only skill is memorizing the rubrics and their newer options. Nor does the answer lie in freewheeling, "relevant" priests who write their own rites.

In order to look sensibly at the role of the clergy, one can speak generally of three proficiencies needed by liturgical leaders, with specific references to the Directory for Masses with Children. As others in this volume point out, it is a basic document for everyone's reflection.

Know the Children

First of all, the priest must be able to live with and to know children and young adults. Good presiding at prayer necessitates a leader who can act and speak with a deep rapport. Every Christian has probably had the unfortunate experience of sitting among congregants who were mentally and spiritually miles away from the person leading them. To lead celebrations with children, it is not enough to say cute things or to quote from television commercials. And we need more than patient smiling at their banners.

Knowing children means appreciating them as they really are in this decade. A romanticized view will not be enough. Priests should try to enter into their pain, fears, and hopes. This does not require forty-year-old pastors to act like eight-year-olds. It may not even involve knowledge of their "in" jokes and jargon. (What does the word "wicked" mean in your parish?) The ambiguities and longings of young parish members should fill and inspire sympathetic adults. As the Directory states: "Today the circumstances in which children grow up are not favorable to their spiritual progress" (no. 1). If the eucharist and other liturgies are to include their full interior participation, the obstacles to young people's spiritual progress should be known. Of course, this knowledge does not come from books or from memories of one's own childhood. As always, the best presiders at liturgy are sensitive, caring pastors who know their brothers and sisters.

Liturgical problems are often problems with the community, not with the rites. This is hardly news to most of us. As much as in any other area of parish life, children's liturgies require pastors who are with the children when someone dies or is baptized or is anguishing over internal struggles. When the young congregation knows their presider from other events, when they have a sense that they can trust him or that he is theirs, then the priest can facilitate, not hinder, participatory worship. Celebrants do not have to be extroverts, mime artists, witty raconteurs, or "hams." First and foremost they must be true and gentle pastors who are one with the assembly.

Know Oneself.

There are times when the pastor is both a good listener and a wise leader. On every front he can relate to young and old. Yet when he stands before a liturgical assembly (adults or children, or both), he freezes. He might put on a "sacred" mask, which he learned at seminary—a tighter or deeper tone of voice, a gaze above all heads, a set of gestures determined by rote rather than the given situation. Beyond a knowledge of the children, celebrants of children's liturgies must know themselves. Again, this is scarcely a surprise, but its practical import is too often ignored. Priests who are uncomfortable with their own bodies are rarely capable of basic and easy gestures. On the other hand, those who know they have a tendency to ramble can discipline their tongues and minds to be brief. Those who are seldom able to find apt applications of the gospel for children can follow no. 24 of the Directory and have an appropriate lay person speak after the gospel. Knowing one's gifts and limits can turn both into assets.

Know the Rites.

Equally important and obvious is a third area of knowledge. The Roman Rite has a particular flow to its calendar and its eucharist. The reforms are now many years old; children who received first communion in the new Mass are now out of high school. While these young people may have internalized the general flow of the reformed celebrations, they may not have had a single experience of its full potential. Their years of growth may have been spent in a small parish where for years the two pastors followed only the letter and not the spirit of renewal.

The local implementation of the fully participatory 1969 Roman Missal has indeed been uneven. Many priests do not have a sense of its internal movement: how one part builds on the former, how a pattern of proclamation-response characterizes the liturgy of the word, and how recommended options can enhance the basic movement from word to eucharist. This lack of knowledge often results if a priest's education and ecclesiology have fostered a legalistic attitude. The Mass becomes a series of parts listed in a mandated missal to be performed in accord with exact rubrics. This focuses the priest's attention on each part rather than on the whole flow of the ritual. Where rubrics are not given in the new missal, old ones persist, making the celebration lawful on the surface but actually lacking in overall coherence.

This is not to suggest that liturgical law is a disposable item. Rubrical knowledge, however, must be a part of an overall perspective, a liturgical sensitivity to the ritual's outline. A priest should know the genre of presidential prayer (opening prayer, eucharistic prayer, etc.). He should be able to adapt the rite so that the children are able to enter the celebration, and to perform this adaptation so that the general structure of the Mass becomes clearer. The Directory (no. 39) points out that some of the texts and rites should not be changed. For example, the response "and also with you" should be kept so that confusion does not arise at every Mass ("What do we say back?"). Building on this, the Directory (nos. 40-54) goes through the Mass and shows how a true understanding of each section can guide the selection of parts to be done or to be omitted.

Besides offering a correct context for the legalists, awareness of the Mass's structure and particular styles can aid those who give high regard to their own whims. Adaptation must enhance internal and external participation. It must respect the gathering of hearts (opening rites), the hearing and responses to the word, the blessing and sharing of the eucharistic gifts, and the sending forth to mission.

A similar sensitivity must be fostered regarding the calendar. Children's lituriges, their adaptations, and homilies should express the seasons of Advent, Christmas, Lent, and Easter. This is not a servile task for planners, but one that can unleash the full potential of the lectionary, sacramentary, and yearly rhythms. Especially in Ordinary Time, planners and clergy can also note other calendars (school graduations, town harvest festivals, etc.)

The care for the liturgy's structure often demands considerable sacrifice. One may have to budget high sums for quality continuing education. Others might find it necessary to allot one morning a week to sequestered reading. Or they may want to invite (and pay for) outside liturgists to visit and evaluate their planning meetings and celebrations.

Perhaps the biggest sacrifice is yet to be mentioned. Priests must learn that good liturgy means sharing roles. A children's liturgy is not a chance for Father to look good in children's eyes. Too often the congregation must politely sit back as the conservative or liberal, young or old pastor "impresses" them. True worshipers know that the priest and "themes" are not there to impress them. Everything in liturgy is meant to foster *expression*.

Two Examples

Building on these three virtues--knowledge of the community, oneself, and the rites—priests can grow spiritually through children's liturgies. They can then face specific problems with a better perspective. Two brief examples follow: how to compose or adapt prayers and how to educate through the liturgy.

The Directory states:

> Above all, the priest should be concerned about the dignity, clarity, and simplicity of his actions and gestures. In speaking to the children he should express himself so that he will be easily understood while avoiding any childish style of speech. (no. 23)

The word "childish" is used in the pejorative sense. On the other hand, the priest's words and adapted prayers should have the direct style, easy vocabulary, and graphic images that communicate with both young and old. Comfort with one's identity as an adult, coupled with a knowledge of a child's comprehension, helps priests who are adapting their language (no. 51). A knowledge of the Mass's structure helps celebrants to stay with the intended genre. One should not lapse into moral exhortation when one is actually trying to conclude intercessions.

This perspective also helps with the liturgy's didactic task. As the Directory reminds us: "the liturgy itself always exerts its own proper didactic force." A prayerful celebration teaches by its experience of common awe, by the word proclaimed, by the kingdom of justice taking flesh in the community. It does not teach through heavy-handed use of themes. Once more, each priest must continue to grow in his sensitivity.

The Directory for Masses with Children does not call on every priest to learn an entire new set of absolute rubrics. Nor does it call on everyone to be a clown. It summons the clergy to their perennial mission to know their people and to know themselves, and thus to lead their assemblies in true worship of God.

SEVEN

MUSIC, GESTURES, AND PICTURES— ALL FOR CHILDREN

Since the Directory for Masses with Children was first published in 1973, we have been implementing its valuable insights. Why, then, do so many of the adults who are facilitating children's celebrations seem to have fallen heir to the job solely because no one else was willing? Certainly, there are fine elementary teachers who love and understand children, and who also love and understand liturgy who have chosen the vocation of raising the quality of the worship life of preadolescent Christians in their parishes. The names of these truly magnificent souls should be submitted to the Holy See for canonization. A word should also be said in recognition of those of us who find our work with children a delightful and rewarding adjunct to our general liturgical ministry.

It is those few saints with vision who were represented by the drafters of Chapter One, nos. 8-15 of the Directory. The insights contained in this chapter are universal and consistent with liturgical formation of Christians of any age. However, the remainder of the document needs rather major revision or expansion to be of real or practical value to those in the field it proposes to direct.

Points of Reference

Despite the shortcoming, there are some seeds of inspiration in various points that are made outside Chapter One. We who are actively involved with children in our parishes would do well to study this document to locate those points of reference. Toward that end, consider each of the first sentences of nos. 30, 33, 35, and 37.

> Singing is of great importance in all celebrations, but it is to be encouraged in every way for Masses celebrated with children, in view of their special affinity for music. (no. 30)

> The development of gestures, postures, and actions is very important for Masses with children in view of the nature of the liturgy as an activity of the entire man and in view of the psychology of children. (no. 33)

> The liturgy of the Mass contains many visual elements, and these should be given great prominence with children. (no. 35)

> Even in Masses with children "silence should be observed at the proper times as part of the celebration" lest too great a role be given to external action. (no. 37)

Almost two decades of liturgical development have elapsed. What could these sentences say that would be of even more value to us now? The four essential thoughts could be updated, changing a few words, to read as follows:

> Singing is *essential* in all celebrations, but it is especially *essential* in every way for Masses celebrated with children, in view of their *natural affinity for music.*

> *The development of gestures, postures, and actions is necessary* for Masses with children, in view of the nature of the liturgy as an activity of the entire *person* and in view of the psychology of children.

> The liturgy of the Mass contains many visual elements, and these *will* be given great prominence *by* children.

> In Masses with children silence *will* be observed, naturally, at the proper times, as part of the celebration when it is called for and framed by the communal recognition of a sacred moment.

To further validate such an exercise, now substitute the word "people" for the word "children." The statements still stand, perhaps even more strongly, as basic tenets of good liturgical practice. With these four seeds in hand, all that is left for us is the detail work and a true spirit of possession of the initiatory process by our community.

A Responsibility of the Whole Community

A discussion of singing, music, gestures, actions, visuals, and silence in celebrations with children cannot be valid without strong reference to the *Rite of Christian Initiation of Adults* (RCIA) and the phenomenal effect it is having on communities throughout the church in America. When the RCIA is fully implemented in a community, the ramifications of Christian education and sacramental preparation for children are earthshaking. A community of believers who come to understand or have defined their own conversion process will find it a relatively easy requirement to share this insight with newly formed Christians of any age. What makes sacraments communal is the coming together of people inspired by a mutual concern for each other. The formation and spiritual progress of new Christians are envisioned by the RCIA as the joint responsibility of *all* the faithful. When we understand this, as communities, the value of specifically initiatory and formative liturgical experiences for children will take on a new importance, and call forth a completely new level of energy and serious study among those who will choose this task for their ministry.

If initiation is about entrance into a community, then the Directory is about entrance into a community of one portion of that community, in one of many ways. A community that takes its responsibility for initiation seriously will not overlook the intrinsic value of gathering children together in free space to hear the word, the traditions and stories of that community, and to share a "meal of friendship" as it is so eloquently described in no. 9 of the Directory. In this experience, the "active, conscious, and authentic participation" of these young people will enable them to become adults who understand and are free within themselves to participate fully and even assume leadership in the worshiping community of the future.

Contemporary sacramental theologians are debating whether

there is one sacrament—the church—or an indefinite number— the ensemble of self-expressive acts of the church's life. Regardless of the outcome of that debate, our investment in the communal experience of our children will be well spent.

Now that we have properly justified our existence, what can we say of a practical nature about the four elements of celebration with children?

Singing and Music

The most practical advice about music in celebrations with children is that it had better be worthwhile and *real*. Somewhere around the age of four, a small human being develops invisible antennae or detectors. As soon as "pretend" music starts, these detectors turn on, the child starts to fidgit, and the child is lost for the duration. "Pretend" music for children is rhythmically dull and unchanging, melodically oversimplified, and set to texts that are either meaningless or false. "Pretend" music for children's celebrations can be good music that is being "led," that is, *performed* by a well-intentioned, shrill-voiced sporano who has taught herself a few chords on the guitar and has an infectious smile. "Pretend" music for children can be good music, well taught and accompanied, but "stuck in" between Father's really important stuff way up there on the altar.

In other words, there is no music that is pastorally, liturgically, and musically sound for the adult community that cannot be used with children, except for reasons of performance difficulty. (There might be a justifiable moment for the "Hallelujah Chorus" at the Easter Vigil, but it would be unlikely that the nine-year-olds could handle that *and* the Easter eggs at 9:30 Mass the next day.) The reverse is not true, of course. There is good music for children's celebrations that would not at all be pastorally sound for adults.

Look for strong acclamations that you can repeat upon first hearing, place a good bass line and keyboard rhythm under them, embellish and vary them (eventually) with small touches as flute, handbells, xylophones, guitars, and whatever else the children can play, and sing those same notes and words *all year*. Let them become a part of the community. Let them be known by heart. Then let the young ministering community sing them naturally and fully, in dialogue with the Christ present among them, with the assistance of the presider.

Find a dozen good strong songs in a variety of styles that can bear up under a variety of accompaniments or even a cappella singing. Systematically, with malice-of-forethought, introduce and repeat and repeat these, in various combinations, until all twelve are known almost as well as "Silent Night." If your children are singing them as they ride their bikes, your plan is indeed working.

Gestures and Actions

Axiom: Children are moving entities. Stillness is unnatural for them, except occsionally when sleeping.

Heretofore we have limited ourselves to stand up/kneel/sit in church. This is vertical behavior. Children are not vertical people. Unfortunately, we have been teaching them and ourselves to become more vertical as we get older and "more spiritual." This trend needs to be reversed.

Children are mostly short. The tall ones tend to sift toward the back. So let us keep them on their feet, in a receptive posture, around the table, around the book, around each other. Let us invite them to join their hands. Let us touch them, and be inviting and receptive to their touching us. If we allow and encourage this kind of intimacy in the liturgical atmosphere, it will be second only to song in bringing about the exerience of community. We are touched far too little in our real lives, and it inhibits our being touched by God in the mystical experience.

Work toward a truly relaxed attitude among the adult leaders, about who may be where, and when. If we continue to regiment straight lines at the banqueting table, we continue to belie our invitation to "break bread together." Obviously there needs to be some order, but not nearly as much as people think.

Finally, there is the question of conscious choreography. How many times can you sign or dance the Lord's Prayer before it loses effectiveness? The answer depends on your community. But just as in music, a little special effort goes a long way with children. When a gesture, such as uplifting hands, is natural and flows out of the real-life experience of the community, it can go on and on. But when a gesture requires continued assistance or special costuming or leadership, it will be used most effectively for special occasions.

Visuals

When all elements come together well in a celebration, what the individual can "see" is multifaceted. The esthetics of the second-grade felt banner can be offset by the gesture of reconciliation between a young boy and his sixth-grade sister as they cooperate in placing the cloth on the table and lighting the candles. The sight of real bread being broken slowly and deliberately so that we can take our portion while singing a refrain that remembers Jesus will offset the cold cafateria floor or the squeaky folding chairs. The pride of communal ownership of a friendship chain made of construction paper that connects all the pews offsets the extremely formal posture of the very uncomfortable presider.

If we use as many real, alive visuals as we can find, in the form of people and plants, and recognize the connecting points to life outside the communities gathering, our eyes will be fed along with our bodies and spirits.

Silence

There are moments in our adult lives when words fail us. There is a sacred space in which to speak would be sacrilege. There is a connection of eyes and hearts that does not need explanation. This experience is also real for children. If *theos* is the root word for theatrical, then so be it.

In our celebrations with children we need never say "Shhh." Quiet will come when quiet is what is necessary. The freedom to celebrate, the whole person, in this community, led by someone who knows a story or a movement that we have never heard or seen, will come together in a profoundly serious moment in which all will be silent. There is an innate respect in all of us for the gift of being lifted, ever so briefly, out of the ordinary and into a higher reality. Children know this better than we do.

EIGHT

WHAT DOES IT MEAN
TO BE A CHILD?

Whenever I think about children in the liturgy, a story from Mark's Gospel immediately comes to mind. One day, when Jesus was teaching, "people were bringing their little children to him, for him to touch them. The disciples turned them away, but when Jesus saw this he became indignant and said to them, 'Let the little children come to me; do not stop them; for it is to such as these that the kingdom of God belongs. I tell you solemnly, anyone who does not welcome the kingdom of God like a little child will never enter it.' Then he put his arms around them, laid his hands on them and gave them his blessing." (Mark 10:13-16)

We have all heard this story many times, but our understanding of children often seems no greater than that of the disciples. In Jesus' day, children, like women, were second class citizens; they could often be traded off like cattle. They were the forgotten of Yahweh. In our own time, children are still misunderstood, still second-class citizens. Like the disciples, we see children as an inconvenience and do our best to turn them away. We urge them to grow up as soon as possible. We don't even seem to have a place for them in our adult religion. We have eucharistic prayers for children, but our church has never developed a real theology of childhood.

Adults do not understand children and children know this. They may be small, but they are smarter and more intuitive than we often think they are. As in *The Little Prince* by Saint Exupéry, they know that children and adults often exist in very different

71

worlds. One day when he was still a child, says Saint Exupéry, he drew a picture of a boa constrictor digesting an elephant. But when he showed it to adults, they all said it was a picture of a hat. And the author comments:

> In the course of this life I have had a great many encounters with a great many people who have been concerned with matters of consequence. I have lived a great deal among grownups. I have seen them intimately, close at hand, and that hasn't much improved my opinion of them. Whenever I met one of them who seemed to me at all clearsighted, I tried the experiment of showing him my Drawing Number One, which I have always kept. I would try to find out, so, if this was a person of true understanding. But whoever it was, he, or she, would always say "that is a hat." Then I would never talk to that person about boa constrictors, primeval forests, or stars. I would bring myself down to their level. I would talk to them about bridge, and golf, and politics, and neckties, and the grownups would be greatly pleased to have met such a sensible man.

It seems we are always asking children "When are you going to grow up?" When was the last time a child asked you "When are you going to become like a child?"?

The Parable of Childhood

Nathan Mitchell has made several observations abut children and childhood that are well worth noting here ("The Parable of Childhood," *Liturgy* 1:3, 1981). The first is that childhood is universal. Not everyone is a husband, a wife, a sister, or a brother, but *everyone* is a child. It is the common denominator shared with every living human being. We may end a marriage, lose a job, or move away from a friend, but we will always remain children.

Second, the Scriptures use many metaphors to speak of the relationship between God and his people. The marriage of God and Israel is one of the most beautiful metaphors in the Old Testament, but as we see in Hosea, even that relationship can be adulterated and severed. Only the metaphor of the bond between God, the parent, and Israel, the child, continues without end.

Even when Israel strayed, God never gave up on his child.

Third, Mitchell reminds us that the focal point of our childness is Jesus, the Son. Jesus is most like a child when he was on the cross. It was there that he was most vulnerable, most reliant on others. On the cross, God is no longer big, but small--as "small and vulnerable as someone's dying child."

Finally, children are parables of God working in the world today. The theme of children runs throughout the Scriptures, but it is especially strong in the Old Testament. God promises Abraham that his descendents would be as numerous as the stars. Speaking through Hosea God says: "When Israel was a child, I loved him, and I called my son out of Egypt . . . I myself taught Ephraim to walk. I took them in my arms . . . I was like someone who lifts an infant close to his cheek, stooping down to him. I gave him food." (Hosea 11:14)

For the Jews, God is Father, and Jerusalem, the city, is mother. And we believe that from this union came Jesus, who tells us that unless we become like little children, we will not experience God.

Four Qualities of Childhood

What does it mean to be a child? There are many ways to answer that question, but I think there are four qualities or characteristics of childhood that are extremely important for us and our liturgies.

The first of these qualities is imagination and creativity. The Directory for Masses with Children (no. 35) states: "The liturgy should never appear as something dry and merely intellectual." This sentence should be tattooed on the back of every parish liturgy chairperson in the country, for our liturgies are often so dry and cerebral that they become headtrips for adults. No wonder children don't want to stay at Mass!

Father Patrick Collins says that:

Liturgy's language is not that of word and concept. It is rather the language of image and symbol. The part of the human person addressed in worship is not primarily the intellect, but the imagination. Faith is initially expresssed and always most effectively celebrated in symbols that speak to the imagination.

Feelings of conversion, support, joy, repentance, trust, love, memory, movement, gesture, wonder--all of these things appeal to our imagination. If you were to ask yourself what in your own conversion process brought you closer to God, I don't think the answer would be the Baltimore Catechism. I don't think you were persuaded by religious arguments. No doubt you came closer to the Lord through the experience of grace stimulating the imagination, calling you beyond the rational world.

The second quality of childhood involves sensuality and sacramentality. Children first begin to assimilate the world through their senses, not through reason. Children are sensual creatures. They are touchers and feelers. And here they have something to teach us. Psychologists are learning what children have always known: that tactile responses are part of who we are as human beings. There are studies showing that people who have dogs and cats and other pets to be fed, loved, played with, and touched, adjust better to life, and have fewer heart attacks, toothaches, and sinus problems than do people with nothing at all to touch.

The Directory for Masses with Children (no. 33) reminds us that liturgy is an activity of the whole person, and the Constitution on the Sacred Liturgy (no. 7) says that the sanctification of humanity is accomplished through signs perceptible to the senses. This means we are saved and sanctified through signs we can see, taste, touch, and hear. Children seem to know this instinctively. They don't want to sit through a verbose liturgy and a dry sermon. They don't want to hear about our faith. They want to *feel* it, *taste* it, *do* it. They want to use their senses.

When I was a child, the Easter Vigil was a profound event for me. I didn't know what was going on, but I did know they were doing everything I liked. They were playing with fire. They were playing with water. They were singing things I didn't understand. He was blowing on the water! He was spashing the water on people! The air was full of smoke. It was dark and it was scary. It was everything that I loved. That was the beginning of liturgy for me.

We still celebrate the Easter Vigil, but now I hear people saying, "Can't we have something for the children instead?" The Easter Vigil *is* for the children. They know it better than you do.

Don't keep them in their pews. Send them down to watch them try to burn down the columns of the church. Put them out front where the priest can sprinkle them with water. And if he doesn't sprinkle them with water, tell them to get up and go down and tell him, "You missed me!" Let's get rid of the balloons, sparklers, and the Sesame Street characters and get back to those grace-filled elements of life—water, fire, smoke, darkness, and light—all those primeval elements that speak to human beings, especially to the children among us.

The third quality is playfulness and leisure. Children are naturally skilled at play. They don't need expensive toys and regimented games. They use their imaginations. Have you ever given a child a toy and then watched as the child ignored the toy and played instead with the box it came in? Adults, on the other hand, have lost that sense of playfulness and imagination. We need expensive toys and planned vacations; we must *work* at having a good time.

A fourth quality of childhood is openness and innocence. Children have a directness for truth. They haven't yet learned to make value judgments; they risk being vulnerable to love others. "A little child will lead them." And if we are a little suspicious, a little hesitant about what God wants for us, look to the children, because they will bring us closer to God.

Children, Liturgy, and Music

Based on what has been said thus far, I would like to make some further observations about liturgy and music with children.

First, one important comment about ritual. Children need ritual. It helps reassure them about their environment and about what is true and false. That's important to remember, because sometimes well-meaning adults change the ritual every time they gather and the children become liturgical schizophrenics.

It is also important to remember that liturgies *for* children are not an end in themselves. They should not be special rites that differ greatly from the order of Mass celebrated by the assembly, for their purpose is to lead children toward celebrating with the adults.

At every liturgy where children are in the majority, there should be some participation by adults. We've all been to children's liturgies where the children did their thing and the adults sat back as if they were at a little league game and said "Isn't that nice." No! Children know when adults are being condescending. They begin to say "I'm on display." They need to see their parents and other adults participating.

When choosing music for celebrations with children, use the same criteria presented in Music in Catholic Worship. Is the music aesthetically good? Is it liturgically sound? Is it pastoral? Always remember that music in any celebration is a vehicle for prayer.

We all know that there is a lot of bad music out on the market. People are getting rich on kiddie music, bubble gum music. And parishes that are trying to reach out to their children often make the mistake of buying this junk. It's what some people call "pretend music." Pretend music is rhythmically dull and unchanging, melodically over-simplified, and set to texts that are meaningless or false, or even sometimes irreverent. (Pretend music can also be good music played or led badly by a soprano who has taught herself three chords on the guitar.) In other words, there is no music that is pastorally, liturgically, and musically sound for adult communities that cannot also be used with children.

One of the reasons we foist bad music onto our children is because we think we don't have the time or the strength to teach them good music. But children have a special affinity for music. They are so open to it that you can often teach them with greater ease than you can adults. Octave leaps are exciting to them. "Sing a New Song unto the Lord," from Worship II, is a good example. It is interesting and the words are direct.

Lyrics are important, but if the words are sometimes obscure, don't worry. Children don't have to know the meaning of every single word. Music is basically emotion—not an exercise of the mind, but a calling forth of a feeling. Children are much more spontaneous about feelings than are adults. And if something needs to be explained, well, that's what rehearsals are for.

Try using Latin with the children. It's part of the liturgy and tradition of the church, and children are naturally attracted to a language filled with vowels. Why not teach them the music of Taizé? They may not know what it means at first, but they'll love the sounds of the music and words.

Rhythm is also important to children. Make it strong and direct, so they will know where it is going. Children love syncopation; they can hit the offbeat far easier than adults can.

Children should be taught to play rhythmic instruments. It can provide one way of getting them involved in the music program. And when using instruments with children, avoid using only the guitar; it doesn't provide enough support or accompaniment for them to follow.

Always remember that music is a servant at the liturgy. It is there to help the children. When the sacredness of life is expressed through the joy of music, a child will understand what words cannot explain.

In summary, to be proficient at planning and executing and praying at liturgy with children, we must first identify and accept the child in ourselves. Open up yourself to the Lord; open up yourself to being a child. And know the liturgy. Keep it simple, sensual, imaginative, and brief.

Saint John tells us:

> Think of the love that the Father has lavished on us, by letting us be called God's children; and that is what we are. Because the world refused to acknowledge him, therefore it does not acknowledge us. My dear people, we are already the children of God but what we are to be in the future has not yet been revealed; all we know is, that when it is revealed we shall be like him because we shall see him as he really is. (1 John 3:1-2)

When we stand before God who created us, we need only say to him, "Abba," and he will say to us, "My beloved children."

NINE

LEARNING DISABLED CHILDREN AND CELEBRATIONS

A number of years ago a local pastor asked me to substitute for his regular organist. Desperate for cash, I accepted his offer. The church still had its organ placed in the old choir loft (they've since "updated" the sanctuary), so I figured I could catch a few winks during the nonmusical portions of the liturgy. This was a vain hope, as it turned out.

Mass had no sooner started than Monica arrived. Monica (not her real name) was a strikingly pretty girl, about nine years old, with short dark hair. She smiled at me and sat down, seemingly paying attention to the action below us. This lasted about thirty seconds, at which point Monica began to rock back and forth in her chair, shuffling her feet on the floor as her body moved. After a couple of minutes of rocking, Monica stood up and moved to another chair, where she proceeded to rock some more. By the end of Mass, Monica had sat in almost every chair in the loft. She had also crawled on the floor, accidentally knocked the organ plug out of its socket during a hymn, and strewn missalettes about in the way that little girls once strewed rose petals during eucharistic processions.

When Mass ended, Monica's mother appeared and apologized, saying that she usually left Monica at home when the family came to church, but that her sitter was ill, and ...

"Don't worry," I said as I picked up the missalettes and bits of paper. "I'm a school psychologist. I've seen lots of children with learning disabilities. By the way, you may need this." It was one of Monica's shoelaces.

We spent some time talking about Monica. Her school had recently placed Monica in a class for children with learning disabilities. Although of average intellectual ability, Monica was several years behind her class in reading and language arts. Her attention span was short, she was very active (obviously!), and she had difficulty doing written work: one might say Monica's handwriting was sloppy and that her work was generally messy. Most important, Monica could not function well in a large group.

Monica's special classroom had seven children, a teacher, and an aide. There were no gerbils, hamsters, or goldfish—they might distract Monica from her work. The problem was that Monica had great difficulty processing material through her auditory channels. She wasn't deaf, but she could not pay attention to auditory stimuli unless those stimuli were reinforced by using Monica's other senses, especially sight and touch and rhythmic sensations. Educationally, this could be accomplished only in the setting described here.

Fortunately, Monica's school had chosen to address itself to her special needs. Unfortunately, her church had not. In fact, Monica's church was probably unaware that she had special needs, for it still required her to attend services that were primarily auditory in nature, and far too long for her short attention span.

Most of us would have no difficulty appreciating Monica's intolerance for lengthly liturgical services. But a few of us might have some difficulty comprehending Monica's inability to deal with auditory stimuli. Imagine yourself in a large church. The lector is reading from the Old Testament, but the public address system has not been turned on; and when it finally is on, the church's acoustics tend to produce resounding echoes that interfere with the spoken word. You decide to pick up a missalette and read the lesson, only to find that the lessons have not been printed in this particular edition. Recently, you conclude, the church's worship committee—forgetting that there are also adults with auditory processing problems—decided not to provide any means whereby those needing to do so could also read the lessons. The result to you is frustration because you've missed the message. Impatiently, you tap your foot, for everyone knows that adults are prohibited from rocking back and forth during the liturgy of the word.

But while you may search for a church where the acoustics are superb and the texts of the readings are available in printed form, things are different for Monica. Monica and other learning disabled children cannot read well enough to follow the lessons with their eyes. And they will always take their auditory processing problems with them, even to acoustical paradises.

For these children, much of what we do in church is meaningless, even more meaningless than it is for some "normal" children. Granted, their attendance and reception of the eucharist and other sacraments will bring an abundance of *ex opere operato* graces to these children, but one would hope that more serious attention to their liturgical environment would give them the opportunity to prepare for and respond to those graces.

How can we help them? One cannot begin to plan liturgies for any children without first reading the Directory for Masses with Children. Most people who get around to reading it are usually astounded by the degree of freedom the Roman Church allows for designing children's liturgies. Mass need only consist of a brief introductory rite or a greeting, one lesson (the gospel with its acclamation), a dialog homily, truncated presentation of the gifts, a specially designed eucharistic prayer with its acclamations, reception of the eucharist, and dismissal. The key to success in children's liturgies is simplification of the rites. This is especially true when children with learning disabilities are the members of the assembly.

Learning disabled children require an environment that exudes simplicity. A small classroom or meeting room is better than a church filled with banners and pageantry. An intimate celebration with no more than ten children, a teacher, a couple of parents, and a priest would be preferable to one at which the entire student body is present. Mass once every two weeks, well prepared, might have more positive results than the questionable practice of herding youngsters into church for daily Lenten Mass.

Because many learning disabled children have short attention spans and auditory processing difficulties, intensive preparation for each liturgy is required. There is no room for surprises. Each step, each action must be prepared. In a sense, each child, the entire group must overlearn their parts.

Here is an example. In planning a liturgy for children, one might deciede to have a spontaneous dramatic acting-out of the story of the Prodigal Son as it is being read by the priest. One might select the most competent and gifted children to carry out this task on the spur of the moment, and the results would be gratifying. Sadly, children with learning disabilities cannot function this way. Their poor motor coordination and distorted body images usually prevent them from acting spontaneously. Learning disabled youngsters involved in such dramatics would have to prepare themselves ahead of time in order to achieve satisfactory results.

Music presents another problem The songs selected will require more rehearsal time than is usual with other children. It might even be impossible to sing entire songs, in which case short refrains would prove invaluable. Rhythmic activities would also require practice because the nervous systems of learning disabled children do not provide them with the intense kinesthesis that most of us take for granted. In addition, if a non-reader is chosen to do a reading, it will be necessary for that child to memorize the selection. If the group requires further visual reinforcement, it may become necessary to draw or paint a mural related to the liturgy's theme. And if the priest presider does not have good rapport with the children, it will be necessary to appoint another adult to conduct the dialogue homily, as allowed by the Directory for Masses with Children.

If spontaneity and exuberance seem to be lacking from this approach to liturgy with learning disabled children, it is because the intention is to tone things down by finding ways to design liturgies that will, of necessity, by more soothing than uplifting. Most learning disabled children have nervous systems that are already too excitable, which probably accounted for Monica's overactivity in the choir loft. By providing these children with soothing liturgical experiences, we can hope that they will eventually learn how soothing the love of Christ can be.

For some time, I've been impressed with a page from Benzinger's *Remember: Liturgy Activity Book* (1975). It reads: "Find a way to explain to me through my other senses what shapes and forms are. Find a way to explain to me through my other senses what textures and consistencies are . . . what colors and hues are . . . what perspective and distance are." For learning disabled children, this must be our task. Once we have provided them with stimuli to engage their most efficient senses, then we shall succeed in showing them who Christ is.

Children's Choirs
Serving the Community

TEN

CELEBRATING THE SOPHISTICATED SONG OF CHILDREN

The year was 1967 . . . the place was San Marco Cathedral in Venice, Italy. I was eleven years old at the time, a member of the Texas Boys Choir. As a little boy chorister, I can remember marveling at the beauty of the music being sung. San Marco Cathedral was a magnificent space in which to sing. The building boasted a reverberation of some nine to twelve seconds. There were many choir galleries interspersed throughout the cathedral, and it was from one of these galleries that I sang of the salvation of God . . . "In Deo Salutare Meo." Though my eyes were supposed to follow the imposing figure of Maestro Vittorio Negri, I could not help but steal a treasured glance at the Byzantine "Christ Pantocrator"—Lord of the Universe. Set within the haze of ancient mosaic, this stunning, almost frightening figure of Christ loomed over the sanctuary, glaring a reprimand at me for taking my eyes off the conductor. "Ah, at last," I thought, "we've come to the last ritornello passage." (Laugh, you may, but this boy soprano knew the meaning of the word "ritornello.")

The boy's and men's choruses echoed Gabrielli's endless "alleluias," one choir to another; each building and crescendoing to a climactic, definitive, and final cadence with a fermata that set a world record for the longest held alleluia. "Stagger breathe!" I recalled. We all knew Maestro Negri's pet choral concepts. While holding the final chord, the maestro surveyed the musicians to assure himself that all eyes from the three choirs, two brass

ensembles, and two organists—further separated sixty feet between galleries— would see his cut off. It was the reverberent
sound after his release that truly exemplified the fabled acoustics
of this twelfth-century Byzantine cathedral.

This Columbia Masterworks recording entitled "The Glory of
Gabrielli" won two Grammy awards, and my experience as a
member of the Texas Boys Choir had a tremendous impact on my
life. I am where I am today because of it. My mother has saved
the postcard that I sent to her from that year in Venice: appa-
rently I was a spoiled brat, complaining about the fishy smell of
Venice, the shock of not having hot dogs, Dr. Pepper, or television. Yes, I was a homesick . . . a growing boy.

Today, as an adult, I can appreciate what I experienced then,
for that intense, worthwhile, and sophisticated training resulted
in my present profession. Without such a background I would
probably be sweeping floors.

As a child, I can remember being intrigued by the human
singing voice. Whenever I heard a singer, I always asked myself:
how can he or she sing so high, or produce such a beautiful sound
with the voice? The first time I heard the Texas Boys Choir sing
in harmony, I was fascinated by the sound. I wanted to be in that
choir. Since the parochial school I attended offered no such program, and the parish I attended had only an adult choir, it was
with a tremendous sense of accomplishment that I passed the
audition and was accepted as a member of the Texas Boys Choir.

After I concluded four years of membership, my late father, Dr.
Feliks Gwozdz, who was director of our parish's adult choir,
decided to include boy sopranos in the adult soprano section at
Sunday Mass. It was an awkward situation, especially since the
music budget was zero, and I had to stand between two very tall,
well-endowed women and share their dilapidated copy of "A
Short Mass" by Noel Goemanne. However, when I became a
seventh grader, my father asked that I form a children's choir.

He sent me to a children's choir seminar given by the re-
nowned Helen Kemp, whose concept of children's choirs fascinated me, especially her use of simple, non-threatening techniques to teach children to sing. She introduced us to a national
children's choir organization called Choristers Guild, whose
main goal was the formation of Christian character through chil-

dren's choirs. After many, many years of forming and directing children's choirs, I can share Choristers Guild's belief that a positive choral experience can be a profound factor in the religious growth of children. Ruth Krehbiel Jacobs, founder of Choristers Guild, points out that "the church school bears responsibility for religious education, but only the choir offers opportunity for expressing beliefs, aspirations, and devotion in public worship."

VALUE OF THE CHILDREN'S CHOIR

In religious education programs today, the fundamentals of the Catholic faith are taught to children in different forms of curricula. Most generally include the teaching of the sacraments, Scripture, and the life of the church. These subjects are taught by a variety of instructors during a child's religious educational development. The teaching and experience of liturgy is usually left up to the individual instructor. As a result, continuity in liturgical instruction is lacking.

Father Thomas Shepard says that "children need ritual. It helps reassure them about their environment and about what is true and false. That's important to remember, because sometimes well-meaning adults change the ritual anytime they gather and the children become liturgical schizophrenics." He further points out that "liturgies for children are not an end in themselves. They should not be special rites that differ greatly from the order of Mass celebrated by the assembly, for their purpose is to lead children towards celebrating with adults."

The children's choir provides a "hands-on" experience of liturgy and, through the guidance of one director, promotes continuity of liturgical instruction that spans the formative years of a child's development.

Music is a fundamental, visible, audible part of the church. Liturgy and music have combined over the centuries to inspire, uplift, and involve people in an active relationship with God. As stated in the Vatican II documents, "Sacred music intimately linked with liturgical action, winningly expresses prayerfulness, promotes solidarity, and enriches the sacred rites in heightened solemnity." Children's choirs continue to play a significant role in that effort as they provide leadership for hymns, acclamations, and responses sung by the assembly, and inspiration through their anthems. We should all be aware of what the Constitution on the Liturgy states about music. "The musical tradition of the Universal Church is a treasure of immeasurable value, greater even than that of any other art. The main reason for this pre-eminence is that, as sacred melody united with words, it forms a necessary and integral part of the solemn liturgy" (no. 112).

Although choir programs in local parishes may vary from single choirs to large, multiple choir systems involving perhaps hundreds of participants, all serve to enrich the life and worship of the parish community. A parish music program is greatly lacking if there is no representation by children. We cannot expect leaders for our liturgical music in the future, or even well-trained singing assemblies, if we do not begin now with the youth of our parishes.

If one were to prioritize, children's or youth choirs should be the first to be promoted and developed in our parishes. Children, in fulfilling the same ministerial role as adults, learn the value of service to the church, and in a tangible way begin to develop a sense of belonging to the community of faith through their choir experience. The texts they sing encourage thoughtful reflection on their faith. The eucharistic celebration becomes more meaningful and enjoyable as choirs learn the mechanics of ritual and assume leadership roles. Regular rehearsals help choirs to develop a sense of commitment to the work of the church. Service opportunities, such as singing at hospitals and nursing homes, can introduce them to additional areas of the church's mission. Fellowship with other choir members and participation in festivals with choirs from other churches can make them aware of the value of being part of the Christian community. The choir director can serve as a model of a responsible, caring Christian adult. It is not surprising that many youngsters have been drawn into active church membership by participating in a choir program.

Before initiating a children's choir program, the pastor and minister of music must first agree that the participation of a children's choir in the liturgy is a desirable priority. If the pastor thinks in terms of exploiting the children as a "cute" addition to the liturgy, or if the music minister thinks in terms of "putting on a performance," the concept should be quickly shelved. However, if it is agreed that the children's choir will play a significant role in the effort to inspire and involve the assembly in an active relationship with God, then the program is ready for take-off.

Today it is vital that a parish children's choir program bear the responsibility of playing a major role in the realm of music education. It is a fact, unfortunately, that most school boards consider music education to be a "frill" item, and many financially-strapped school systems have trimmed their music programs drastically. I have heard nightmare stories of justifications for music programs at schools. Many such classes are established as periods to baby-sit the students during the teacher's breaks.It is common that such programs exist on a zero budget, and may end up as "sing-along" sessions. On the other hand, we often hear of wonderful music education programs in some dioceses and of school districts that have developed music curriculum guidelines. But these are exceptional situations. In the majority of cases, it is left to the parish musician to take steps to ensure the growth and development of church music programs well into the distant future.

In today's Catholic parish, children are divided into two groups in the area of education: those that attend public schools and those that attend the parochial school. The establishment of a children's choir program should serve to unite both groups, especially in terms of scheduling rehearsals, Masses, and other fellowship activities.

Children's choirs must be trained by qualified directors at regular, weekly rehearsals. Young singers are intrigued by the voice, and are eager to learn the basic vocal production that leads them from fine unison singing to part singing. Since parish choir membership combines children from both public and parochial schools, directors will encounter all levels of musical accomplishment. As I have said earlier, schools may or may not be providing some of this instruction. It is an important responsibility of the choir director to know each child's level in the area of both vocal and musical education development.

THE INTERVIEW

The practice of letting every youth choir applicant into the choir without first interviewing him or her can make the director's job more difficult. An interview session—not to be confused with an audition—gives the director an opportunity to meet both child and parent before membership acceptance. At such interviews, such vital information as name, address, telephone number, and date of birth are documented. Expectations and membership "re-choir-ments" are also made clear to the parents. For example, in our parish each child is expected to attend on a weekly basis:

1. Wednesday rehearsals—5:30-6:45p.m.
2. Sunday warm-up—11:30a.m.
3. Sunday Mass—12:00 noon.

It is emphasized to the parent and child that these activities will be re- "choired" if the child is to be accepted as a committed choir member.

To help ensure a very successful children's choir program, I go a step further to ensure committment from both parent and child. I call it follow-up. The follow-up policy is mainly conveyed to the parents: if the child has to miss any of the required activities, the parent must call our *choir excuse line* (my personal home answering machine) before the activity that the child will miss. Failure to call the excuse-line will be recorded as an unexcused absence. After two unexcused absences, the membership contract is then terminated.

In addition, I point out that the following reasons for absence will not be accepted. *No transportation.* This is a parental responsibility. Of course, flat tires, car accidents, and flash floods are the exceptions. Another common absence that I consider unexcused is *too much homework.* The choir child is expected to work around the times required to be a member. If this becomes a problem, it is recommended that the child drop out of choir. *Sports activities*are notorious for conflicting with such church activities as choir. It is not unusual for the parent to explain that the coach has scheduled an all-important game and, if Johnny is not in attendance, he will be kicked off the team. In response to the parent, I point out that the coach of the choir team also requires Johnny to be in attendance at choir, and I further remind the parent of our *follow-up policy.* It is at this interview session that I clarify any potential rehearsal conflicts such as sports, piano lessons, and dance activities. As a result, most parents seek out activities that will not conflict with choir requirements.

The next part of the interview session is listening to the child's voice. Easy vocal exercises determine the child's range; rhythms are echoed through imitative clapping patterns, and pitches are matched—either between piano and child, or the child's and the director's voice. It is during this portion of the interview that the director can recognize the child's level of music education. The child with no vocal training whatsoever sometimes does not know how to match pitch. Unfortunately, some unqualified director will label this child a monotone, forever discouraging this child from singing. Usually these children are *conversational* singers. They have not yet discovered the difference between their singing and their speaking voices. Helen Kemp encourages children to think of singing and speaking as two of four different "channels." The "singing channel" has a lighter, brighter sound and feel than the "speaking channel." The other two channels of a child's voice are whispering and shouting.

Whatever the reason a child cannot match pitch, he or she is accepted for a five-month trial membership period. By this point, ninety-eight percent of pitch problem cases are resolved.

The final part of the interview session is the signing of the contract of commitment by the parent. This ensures that both the parent and child understand the expectations, requirements, and follow-up policy in order to be a member of the children's choir for one season.

Interview sessions are conducted once a year. All members, current and new, are interviewed each year. This annual practice evaluates the growing child's progress in terms of past attendance and vocal range changes.

This process of interviewing to ensure commitment can be applied to all church ministries. A contract of commitment, be it to a choir, a religious education class, or other liturgical ministries, such as lector and eucharistic minister, serves to promote a concrete understanding between the program director and those desiring enrollment. Expectations, requirements, follow-ups, and terms are conveyed and understood. As a result, one will find consistency in attendance and commitment to the program.

THE REPERTOIRE

A vital part of maintaining a children's choir is the repertoire being sung. The repertoire must reflect its sacred liturgical function. The young choristers must be nourished by the *quality* music of the church. The early school years of children are very important in forming the tastes of youngsters, for, as adults, they will appreciate the music with which they are familiar and have heard or sung before. There exists a wonderful opportunity to present the best music to our assemblies by teaching it to youngsters who are often free of the prejudices of adults.

When one chooses music, one should use the same criteria presented in Music in Catholic Worship, published by the Bishops' Committee on the Liturgy. We all know that there is a lot of poor quality music out on the market. Some companies are doing very well financially on what Tom Shepard calls "kiddie music." And parishes that are trying to reach out to their children, whether they are involved in the children's choir or in religious education programs, often make the mistake of buying this—for lack of a better word—junk. Such music is often chosen because it appears quick and easy to learn, it requires less energy to teach than "good" quality music, and the text can *relate* to the kids. An example: read this text that was sung as a closing hymn for a school liturgy.

> Give me gas for my Ford,
> keep me trucking for the Lord.
>
> Give me umption for my gumption,
> keep me function, function, function.
>
> Give me oil for my lamp,
> keep me burning, burning, burning.
>
> Give me salt for my fritos,
> God is neato, neato, neato.

For curiosity reasons, I asked some of the boys and girls in attendance at this school liturgy for their reaction. All agreed that the song in question drew their attention away from the Mass; most thought it was a joke; it fact, everyone in the school that day had fun coming up with their own even more sarcastic verses. Children *know* when something does not belong.

The young singer has a tremendous capacity to appreciate a broad range of styles, from the classics of the masters to the contemporary liturgical music of today's composers. In my experience, children have little difficulty learning Latin anthems, and even Gregorian chant. The success of singing chant depends entirely on *how* it is presented and rehearsed. It should not be singled out as something difficult, unusual, or from the Twilight Zone. The children's choir repertoire must not be based on gimmicks but on proven quality music from all periods: chant to contemporary music.

THE DIRECTOR

Throughout this article I have stressed the need for a qualified director of children's choirs in the parish. It is a mistake to think that just anyone can direct children's choirs in the church. A true incident occurred when a Mrs. Smith begged her pastor to initiate a children's choir in the parish for her daughter. The pastor suggested that she start the choir herself, and further encouraged her to be its director. The well-intentioned parent, challenged by her pastor's misguided encouragement, took on the job, although she knew nothing about music, or even how to sing. This unqualified director was sure that she would learn as she "experienced" the formation of this program. The program collapsed in a matter of months. (I am sure there are similar stories in the appointing of teachers in the religious education field.)

But what are the qualifications required of a children's choir director? It is a job that demands a appreciation and love of children and youth, and a sensitivity to their stages of development. Training in vocal music, choral performance, conducting, music theory, and music history are fundamental. The ability to play the piano or organ could prove to be a great asset. Organizational and planning skills are a must. Even more important, the experience and understanding of the liturgical role of the choir is a much-sought, and sometimes hard to find, qualification of a children's choir director.

Belonging to a children's or youth choir can become an integral part of a young person's life. We need to promote such a vital art. Children's choirs are essential if our rich Catholic heritage is to be maintained, and if our expectations of a growing singing assembly are to become a reality.

ELEVEN

ENTHUSIASM IN CHILDREN' CHOIRS

Building a strong liturgical and musical structure in a child's world is one of the most important tasks of the church in the years before us. Not only is it a right and good thing to do, but also, it is essential to the life and spirit of the church for future generations. For a child, music is a vessel through which the spirit flows naturally. Music plants the seeds of education and expression, which come to fruition not only in the immediate seasons, but also for a lifetime. We must attend our children with great care. We must be sure that what we give them is understandable to them, relevant to their spiritual and social world, and of good quality, since it is to serve as a foundation for their youth and adulthood.

QUALITY AND SUITABILITY

Quality does not mean difficulty or complexity. Rather, it means challenge with purpose. Our goal is the skillful selection of music that will educate, inspire, and enrich the child's life. Often there is confusion between what is child-like and what is childish. Adapting scriptural reading from a children's Bible or setting texts to popular musical styles does not guarantee relevance for the child. Children's needs are quite different from our own because their experiences lead to immediate and spontaneous responses. The early years of development are so important that we cannot put children aside in any regard. They are our own future. If we inspire them only with superficial surges of participation and infatuation, they will lose interest not only in music, but also in the church.

The church should lead us to that which is sacred. The Mass is the common, sacred table for sharing and participation. Is there a way to define what is really sacred and musically suitable for use in the Mass? Putting Scripture to any melody or rhythm does not insure its sacredness. We are not singing to entertain ourselves or a congregation. We are singing to serve and share our best for the Creator. It is not always necessary to be formal, but a sacredness must always be expressed in litrugical music, whether folk or Gregorian. A child feels the spiritual quality of participation without always understanding the inner evaluations. When the sacredness of life is expressed through the joy of music, a child understands what words alone cannot explain.

There are no set rules that automatically insure that the sacred will be experienced through music. All our situations are different. We are different individuals with different backgrounds. We can, however, move forward with our goals and look honestly within to see if we are sharing the sacred part of our musical selves.

ENTHUSIASM

What are some of the goals and methods that have been of value for children and their liturgical participation?

Enthusiasm is the first and foremost key to success for any program with children. Enthusiasm is not only zest, energy, and activity. It is something of far greater importance. Enthusiasm comes to us from the Greek *enthoussiazo,* meaning to infuse with divine spirit. Children are full of that inspired energy, and it is our special opportunity as pastoral musicians to help them realize and maintain their enthusiasm through song. To clarify musicianship and its liturgical effectiveness, there are three areas in which our enthusiasm should concentrate.

Creative expression within a child's understanding. Words and pictures are basic to communication, yet as musicians we use words and sounds. Since words become familiar by a contextual process, they can easily be misused and misunderstood. Words such as *praise, redeemer, mercy* and *glory* bring a large variety of abstract meanings to our mind. How can they be interpreted effectively for a child? A director could review the music of the past season and ask the following questions:

1. Did I take time to explain these words when the choir was learning the music?
2. Did the children of the choir understand the words in their own context so that the music was not a rote repetition of text?
3. Were any of the children able to retain the words in their own minds and vocabularies?

A good way to evaluate the depth of text understanding is by asking the choir these three questions:

1. Have any choir members *seen* this word before?
2. Have any choir members *used* this word before?
3. Can any choir member *express* the meaning of this word?

When a word is known by the mind and understood with the heart, it becomes an integrated tool for the child. To sing with that kind of understanding is essential for true Christian teaching of music. After the text is understood, then it can be clearly articulated to those who are listening. The combination of proper diction and inner understanding allows that creative expression of the child to integrate with the natural and emotional responses within. Look at this simple phrase:

Sing   Al - ie - lu - ia   to the   Lord.

R-33, Choristers Guild

The text is simple and the tune is simple, but the meaning is profound. How can a child best understand an Alleluia? Try defining the meaning in rehearsal without words. With uplifted hands, the bright and smiling eyes, standing tall and lifting our hearts to God, we can express that definition better than we could with words. Singing with the same inner lift brings understanding to the children as well as to the adult congregation.

Here is an adapted Scripture that can be used in the Mass:

Consider the lilies and how they grow
Blossoming there in the field,
'Tis not for their labor they flourish so,
Flowers of beauty to yield.
Through the grace of God above,
Tending all in constant love,
Every want shall be supplied,
For God the Lord will provide.

Natalie Sleeth

—reprinted with permission from Choristers Guild, A-95

The poetic gracefulness of this text adaptation (from Matthew 6) makes the text easy to learn. Words like *consider, flourish, yield, grace,* and *tending* need special attention in rehearsal. The nature of the melodic line, its compatibility with the text, and its gentle appeal make the music liturgically and educationally useful. When the text and melodic line fit together, the sacred possibility can be fulfilled by the enthusiasm of the director and the choir.

Creative clarity of musical concepts. Creative clarity comes from a practical ability to see the abilities of children. Any group that meets only once a week for twenty minutes can only fulfill its potential when the limitations are creatively recognized. Many church music programs have died of "if onlys . . . —if only there was more time to rehearse, if only there was more money in the budget, if only we had a good organ, if only there were no schedule conflicts . . . This list is endless. *If only* we appreciated the truly exceptional musical and educational situations we all have! Truly, creativity comes through the process we use to educate and inspire our choirs musically.

In a beginning situation, there is always the tendency simply to "have the kids sing something" and hope that a love for music will catch on. Unfortunately, this process is the weakest and least effective. A child needs to participate in a creative manner from the very first contact with a director. Whether there are three or forty children, and whether they have tuned voices or breathy, untuned voices, they can still share and participate in liturgy. It is only when choirs have to "perform" that we lose the pastoral attitude that is at the center of worship. Start a beginning choir with the beginning musical elements. Read hymns, Scripture, or an anthem text in rhythm. Start with biblical stories in rehearsal that can be read in an antiphonal or responsorial manner For very young singers, short prayers or echo Scriptures may be useful.

Often when young children do not sing well after a rehearsal or two, we feel either that they are not talented or that they are just not interested. This is hardly true. To read, we must go over the alphabet and basic vowel sounds hundreds of times. A child does not just go easily into good singing techniques without proper psychological preparation. For instance, as we know, warm-ups are important for the voice. But if children do not understand why they are important, and have no immediate proof of their effectiveness, they will become bored by them. Boredom or "lack of enthusiasm" at the beginning of rehearsal results in a much lower level of productivity and creativity for the remainder of the rehearsal. Remarking that tennis players and baseball teams must warm up their bodies before playing helps a child see that the choir members are also physically preparing their bodies and voices for a good and healthy musical sound.

Techniques concerning rhythm, diction, dynamics, and tone quality are all essential. But particular concern with musical contours or subtle essences in the music should not come before its proper time. Lift a choir from where it is to where it should be. Start at the beginning and never forget the child's inner participation and expression. This is enthusiasm on a director's part.

Sacred offering in worship. The liturgy of the word and the liturgy of the eucharist form the center of our corporate Christian experience. Music has the potential to add a great dimension to these experiences. On the other hand, it can also detract from worship and make it seem repetitive. When music, education, and worship become an integrated experience that unifies within a child, then a wholeness matures.

There are many parts of the Mass that can be sung by children. Familar parts of the ordinary fall into place naturally when children join the congregation. The offertory and communion are places for special musical selections, as well as the entrance song. Using choirs for the prelude and postlude is also effective. Taking time to plan the nature of the music with the priest so that it maintains the liturgical focus of each Sunday will strengthen the enthusiasm of the children and the congregation.

Invest in the musical and spiritual lives of children. They will bear fruits of our efforts. Valuable tools are available for developing children's choirs. Among the best is the Choristers Guild *Letters,* the monthly publication of inspiration and "how-to" ideas. Look for local workshops and national events that deal with children's liturgy and music. There is a challenge to meet today, so don't wait till tomorrow.

Permission for texts and music used in this article from Choristers Guild, P.O. Box 38188, Dallas,TX 75238

Dolores Hruby

TWELVE

WHAT ABOUT CHILDREN'S CHOIRS?

"Dad, I like to play football, but I'd rather be in the choir." This isn't a choir director's fantasy; it actually happened. A healthy, athletic, fourth-grade boy said it and broke a football coach's heart. The boy wanted to sing in the fairly new Junior Choir of St. Jude's Church.

We American Roman Catholics don't have a strong, clear tradition of children's choirs. In the pre-Vatican II days, the children in Catholic schools sometimes sang a daily Mass in Latin; sometimes they were part of a beautiful Holy Thursday pageant and processed around the church singing *Pange Lingua*; sometimes in Polish parishes the fifth or sixth grade class would sing for funerals; but a choir of children outside the classroom was a rarity.

In the musical confusion of the immediate post-Vatican II days, all choirs suffered. But now we are seeing a marvelous resurgence of adult choirs and the exciting beginnings of children's choirs in our churches, with their responsibilities newly defined, each filling new and different needs.

RECIPROCITY OF SERVICE

In children's choirs particularly, there is a reciprocity between the child and the parish. The parish is served by the child, and the child is served by the parish. How does the children's choir serve the parish? We are not talking about the Vienna Boys Choir with its daily choir school of highly selective voices. Rather, we are talking about all volunteers accepted, fourth grade and up, who meet for forty-five minutes to an hour once a week. Some of the new volunteers in the younger children's choir cannot match pitches or carry a tune. The overall tone in this choir is less than perfect. Yet they bring sincerity and eagerness, plus hope for the future, which is exciting. To hear what happens to these young singers in the course of a year can bring a feeling of satisfaction in their growth to the whole parish family. As these choir members mature and progress, they can and do add a real dimension of beauty to the liturgies they serve.

These choirs can be combined with the adult choir on special occasions such as Thanksgiving, when there is only one liturgy for the day. There is quite a good selection of music available for SATB or SAB with junior choir. The adult and junior choirs can be used antiphonally. The contrast of timbres with an imaginative use of space can produce a beautiful effect.

The parish serves the children by its appreciation of what the children do; by its financial support of the enterprise; and by recognizing that the choir represents an invaluable religious and musical education for their children. The children are taught from the beginning that their job is to serve the parish. Whenever one says this to them, their eyes mist over and they stand a bit taller. This orientation in children seems to be something rarely tapped and, of course, could be overdone.

"Your job is to help all the people in church." How? One way, since they are in front of the congregation, is by their example. They can help by reverently speaking the spoken parts with the whole congregation; by singing all the hymns and acclamations with gusto; and finally, by singing their anthems as well as possible, understanding that all of these are prayers.

PERSONAL GROWTH

"Sing with Moses and the people," says one of their anthems. Who is Moses? Who are the people? What does it mean? You can't sing a prayer unless you understand it. To this end, they discuss the meaning of the words, so that their knowledge and understanding (as well as that of the director) are increased and reinforced.

"We're going to learn this anthem for Advent." When is Advent? What is Advent? What does it mean? Amazingly, there are many adults who do not know the answers to these questions; they only vaguely recognize the beauty of the church year. The choir children more than know it; they experience it. The liturgy becomes much more interesting to children when they take an active part in it. They enjoy their role of leadership; they understand this idea of commitment. They know that their choir rehearsal is more important than a skating party; they know that it is necessary that each member be there on a given Sunday morning. They respond to this sense of responsibility.

Our children come from six different schools. At first they come as "St. Jude Kids" or "Hills and Dales Kids" but soon they are thinking of themselves as the Junior Choir or Chorister Kids. Serving in the choir develops a sense of unity, a sense of true community.

One happy by-product is that the parents come to experience a deeper unity also. Parents with children in the various schools meet; inactive parents are sometimes drawn into the parish life through their children's choir activity.

Since these children come from so many schools, their musical training varies greatly. A few schools have excellent music programs; some have little or no musical program. The ability of the children to read music must be one of the prime targets of the choir director. For a few choir members, this part of the program is reinforcement; for most, it is an essential ingredient, since it is a skill they do not have.

Helping the child to "find" his or her voice is also important. Again, very few children come with a well-developed soprano tone. Most of them come with a chesty, campfire-song tone that won't take them much above B^1. It certainly is not a suitable range or tone for all the excellent literature available for children's choirs. So a good deal of time is spent on learning to sing properly. But, as Helen Kemp says, this kind of training will give them a musical instrument for life.

When that high voice has been released, and when they begin to understand the early rudiments of reading music, there is so much beautiful music they can sing. A collection of folk hymns; a Bach anthem with flute and organ; a contemporary setting of a psalm with a syncopated beat; a three-part canon that opens the door to part singing; a lyrical anthem with Orff instruments; a song that calls for liturgical dance; all these and more are there for them to experience and enjoy.

There are just a few things that a children's choir should not be asked to do. Those light, high voices cannot lead a congregation in song. They can lead by example, but not by sound. Nor should they be asked to sing every Sunday. This places too great a burden on them and does not allow the director in the limited rehearsal time to teach that which is necessary for them to grow and mature musically.

REHEARSALS

It is my experience that children do not want the choir practice to remind them of the classroom. I came from the classroom into the choir room and had some major problems as a result. But I was fortunate to join Choristers Guild, an excellent, non-profit organization devoted to helping directors of children's choirs. I attended a summer seminar where the grande dame of children's choirs, Helen Kemp, was teaching. It turned my approach to the whole subject 180 degrees around. Much of what I present is culled from reading the Choristers Guild *Letter*, and observing or exchanging ideas with other choir directors. One does not have to slavishly follow every idea one encounters through this avenue, but it opens doors to creative thinking. The following suggestions are the result of years of experience, experimentation, and exposure to Choristers Guild.

How do you start the rehearsal? I slowly drum ten times on a hand drum. All the children who are not yet ready scurry to get their music and be in their seats before the last stroke sounds. Soon they are asking if they can do the drumming, so this also presents an opportunity to show each one how to use the hand drum properly. (And incidentally, when they scurry to those seats, the boys are scurrying to the middle of the group. I have them there so I can respond more quickly to them.)

Immediately we go into some sort of movement to get the body ready to sing. It cannot be emphasized too strongly that the body is your instrument. Sometimes we jog in place, or pick apples from a tall tree, or touch the stars, and the like.

Next, posture must be checked. Both feet are firmly on the

ground; knees slightly bent; body stretched tall; shoulders re-laxed and loose; head held high with a relaxed jaw. To achieve this we sometimes stretch our arms high above our heads, then slowly lower the arms, but no other part of the body. Or pretend that you are a puppet, with someone holding you up by the hair on the crown of your head.

We do some breathing exercises. Inhale, blowing up the balloon inside you, around your waist. Exhale slowly on sssssssss. Or have the children echo you on strong ch-ch-ch-ch sounds in specific rhythms. Or bark like a dog. Feel free to invent your own exercises.

We exercise the head voice by imitating sirens or yodeling, then we go into some simple vocalises. I use one of my hand puppets to illustrate that the mouth should be *open* and that the jaws should be *down*.

We then start rehearsing an anthem. I try to use the anthem for more than just singing. The opening two notes of "A Star, A Star" by Hal Hopson make an excellent vocalise: I start lower (f to b flat) and take it as high as the children can easily sing it. Or use the opening notes of "O Sing unto the Lord" to learn intervals.

Children should not sit still for a whole rehearsal, so I alternate learning anthems with some sort of movement such as echo-clapping, going to the chalk board for various activities, and breaking up into teams to independently work out the rhythm of a new anthem.

I try to illustrate musical ideas with concrete symbols: a cloud I made to show how a held note is lifted; a toy air balloon to exemplify a light tone; a bear bouncing on a wire coil to keep a musical phrase that starts low from getting heavy and chesty.

I keep on index cards ideas I've read or observed, and I add to these and reread them regularly. I'm constantly looking for ideas. Recently I bought a book of musical games and found *one* game that I feel I can use. Therefore it was a good investment. I haunt toy stores for toys that will illustrate a musical point. We must do everything we can to keep rehearsals fun; to keep the children's interest lively.

The work we are doing with children is important. The children's choir gives to the parish an added sacred dimension; to the children it gives a sense of service and commitment as they

actively participate in the liturgy, which they more fully understand because of their participation; it gives them a taste of the
diverse and thrilling sacred music literature; a sense of unity in
community; it provides a sense of excitement in their religious
experience. And for the future church, it holds the promise of a
liturgically knowledgeable, actively singing people.

Music Education
Foundation for
a Singing Community

Robert Haas

THIRTEEN

MUSIC EDUCATION AND THE PARISH: A DREAM

I think it would be helpful if you knew a little bit about me. I began my formal musical education at the age of eleven, and soon after began playing the organ in church. Ever since that time church music and my faith have been important parts of my life. My experiences include being chapel musician and entertainer while in the army during the Korean war. I was a parish musician and organist for many years before and after being in the service. In addition to my experience and love of church music, I have been involved in variety shows, jazz and dance bands, operettas and musical comedy, radio programs, and recitals. I have developed music education programs. I have had a special love and involvement in teaching music, piano, theory, and harmony for some thirty-five years. It is out of this wide variety of musical experiences and teaching that I propose to share with you some of my concerns, feelings, hopes, and dreams about the future of music in the Roman Catholic Church and how it helps shape the future of our children as people who try to live the Gospel.

I would like to reflect on nine areas of concern and rationale for my assertion that music education is and should be the responsibility and concern of the parish and the parish's religious education program.

1. Due to the decline of music education in public and private schools, the parish has the opportunity and responsibility to be a forum for the musical development of its children.

2. Unlike many academic music programs, the church can be a place where any child, regardless of his or her level of musical talent and ability, can experience and take part in music making.
3. Music, more than anything else, is *formational*, and contributes to the prayer and faith life of children. It has the ability to lead them to their liturgical worship life.
4. Music contributes to the *whole* person. It helps us express our creativity, our feelings, and it enables us to express what we believe.
5. Music can help build acceptance and bonding with one another in peer relationships, and, in a faith setting, can help diminish and dispel destructive competition.
6. Through music children can experience themselves as being important in the eyes of the church; they themselves can "evangelize" and renew the church through their enthusiasm and involvement.
7. The church has a responsibility to form and shape our music ministers for the future of our parishes.
8. Music has the potential to help children as well as adults to pray, and to come to know Jesus in a deeper way.
9. The people who are charged with the task of this musical formation of the child need to develop unique characteristics and qualities that will be a positive witness to the child.

Let us now looks at each of these in greater depth.

The Parish: Forum for the Musical Development of Its Children

Throughout this country the arts are not high priorities in our educational systems. This means that, more and more often, music, art, and the humanities are being cut completely from academic curricula. This is dangerous news indeed, for we know through many psychological and educational findings and developments that the arts are critical in the development of the whole person. The imbalance of education that rests solely on the more intellectual rather than the experiential is producing and manipulating a generation of children who are finding it difficult to be creative and to express their feelings. We are also finding that music is something that is not being fostered with great support in the home.

The consequences of this continual lack of emphasis on music and the other arts should force all of us to look beyond the present moment. Our history shows clearly that the Roman Catholic Church has always been at the forefront of artistic activity. The church was the source of some of the greatest compositions and contributions to our musical treasury, and was the financial supporter of some of the greatest of the musical masters. For the society, then, the church was more than Sunday Mass; it was a way of life and the center of life for the community. In a former day, music in the home was a focal point for the family, the scene of families and friends gathered around the piano was part of the fabric of their lives, regardless of their musical ability. The church has a great responsibility and challenge not to let these wonderful traditions die.

The parish religious education program is the ideal place for this musical heritage and training to be developed and fostered. I have experimented with this when I taught in a parish CCD program, where I offered guitar and music classes in addition to the religion part of the program. At my home parish of Saint Christopher's in Bridgeport, Michigan, my students performed recitals that were held in the church itself. I tried to help these students understand that the church was more than a place in which to worship; it was a place for them to share their gifts, a place where they could revel in and celebrate the gifts that God had given them, and to share that with a community of family and friends who care for them and love them. Our Protestant brothers and sisters are much better at this than we are; their various choir schools and music programs can serve as models of what could be for us Catholics.

The Parish: Place Where Children Can Experience Music-Making

Very often I have had the experience of hearing friends say that they wished they could do music, but cannot, because years ago some teacher told them they couldn't sing, or that they were not as good as somebody else. We know people whose self-esteem was bestroyed by being told this. We also hear stories of persons who were deprived of music when they were young because their parents could not afford lessons or an instrument. If economics becomes the trump card for whether or not children can experience the bauty of music, if musical talent alone determines whether or not the child is allowed to make music, then the assertion that music is the universal language is a lie.

For too long we have been too lazy to see the musical potential in all children. We too quickly make the judgment that a child is tone deaf, that a child has no talent, often to the destruction of the child and the gift that is probably hidden deep within. As Emmet Wilson says in *How to Help Your Child with Music*:

> Any normal child can learn to play an instrument. Every normal child learns to talk though the mechanism of the voice may require more sensitive control. Some children do not learn to talk as early as others; some may not be great orators or distinguished actors. These differences or limitations might be explained as talent, or a lack of talent in the art of speech. But no one would question a child's ability to learn to talk effectively despite the lack of such talent. The case is no different with music. Some children will take to music at a much earlier age than others; some never can become great singers or virtuosos; but any normal child can learn to play. The question of talent need not be considered until the child has become more than a satisfactory performer on his or her chosen musical instrument.

What is needed, and the parish can be the place for this, is an environment where that individual child can be affirmed and formed in the musical journey. What is needed is a wholistic and patient musical approach where music is experienced in a loving and supportive community, where the pure joy of music is valued rather than what degree of advanced skill or performance is attained. The child needs to develop a sensitivity as an experienced listener or performer. The individual needs to be promoted, not forced to submit to some prescribed set of requirements. We need a non-pressured approach that constantly communicates to the child that his or her particular level of musical expression and enthusiasm is of high value. This mindset is valuable regardless of the subject being presented—the children feel you are working with them directly and singularly. In practical terms, the basics of this are very simple: a proper and genuine eye contact with the child shows how sincere you are, and having the ability to see what is there in that little face. It means perhaps beginning your time together with an opportunity for the children to express and share what is on their minds that day, what has been happening in their lives since you last saw them. This can help promote an atmosphere that does not hold up standards to them that may intimidate them or suppress their desire to learn and play.

The Formative Power of Music

Music has the power to form and shape all of us. It influences what we believe, and challenges and prods us to go further than we have. As we know in the liturgy, music helps us to pray. It greatly intensifies our worship. To *not* have music in the liturgy is to do the liturgy a disservice; plainly it means that we are not really doing liturgy. We know the influence that music, particularly pop and rock music, has had on the youth of this country and throughout the world; we know that it has shaped and molded their culture and still does. We know how music and its message can bond people together, especially when we look at music of the Black tradition during the civil rights era. It was music that helped unite those people and their cause. It helped them articulate what words alone could not do. We experience the power of music throughout our world and our human experience. The church is also about bonding people together around the Lord Jesus, to become a community of believers trying to build a better world. Music, in other words, is one of our best and most effective teachers. When children are nourished through music during their growing years, it shapes and molds them socially and personally. The Christian message of love, peace, justice, and forgiveness, when sung, has the power to penetrate the child's memory and attitudes in a way it cannot when it is just read or shouted from some textbook.

The basic message here is that music has proven to be a form of communication that we cannot ignore. It has power. It speaks volumes beyond many other forms of communication. The challenge to implement music creatively has an integral part in the formation of our children, in their faith and in their lives, and in their culture as human beings throughout all the stages of their development.

Music Contributing to the Whole Person

Music frees us to express who we really are—our uniqueness, our gifts, our distinct personalities. We live in a world that is often critical of being unique, a world that often prefers and encourages uniformity and conformity, that discourages individual thinking and creativity. Music here can serve as a healing source, one that can help us to cry, to feel joy and sorrow, to express our love and excitement. Music can also be an expression that helps the children to come to know their bodies through movement, rhythm, and singing, which helps the music to be experienced as something they embody, rather than something they just recite. Music helps us mark the journey of our life and development, and helps embody a vision for the future. Music can express what we most want and desire, and it can enable us to sing about what it will be like on that day where there will be no hate and destruction, when we will live in peace.

Music Helping Build Acceptance and Bonding

Competition is not always a bad thing. It can often be a great contribution to the development of the child's character. But more often than not, it has resulted in some very destructive aspects of the child's self-esteem and enthusiasm, especially in sports and in the arts. Most school music programs fail in dealing with these problems, and too often this leads to a great loss of self-confidence in the child, not just in music, but in many other aspects of their lives, which can cause a separation between children and their peers rather than bringing them closer together. As Jesus said, "You who wish to be first must be last and the servant of all." Those of us who possess talent need to serve and affirm those who may not seem to have acquired the highest degree of excellence. We need to bond ourselves to those children who feel alienated or separated from those who seem to have made it. Music calls us to associate ourselves with all of the children, not just those who happen to have a high degree of accomplishment. In this context, music does not exist for its own sake. It is to be a vehicle to help children experience themselves as a community, as the body of Christ.

Music Integrating Children into the Church

One of the attitudes that all of us need to constantly rid ourselves of is the notion that our children are the *future* of the church. They are the church *right now*. They have the same status as adults and hold their own unique wisdom that contributes to the life of the church and gives witness to the presence of Christ throughout the world. We diminish their worth and status in many ways—by depriving them of participation in liturgical ministries, by not encouraging them to become involved in the parish, and worst of all by creating liturgical experiences for them that separate them from the rest of the worshiping community. We deepen their second-class status by giving them so-called "children's music" to sing. We keep them from singing the hymns and songs of our tradition, and give them only the sappy kiddie music that does not contribute to their growth, but keeps them in a prison that encourages separation.

At the same time, to shove them into the adult experience without providing them with musical and liturgical opportunities where they can express themselves in their own unique way is to cause equal damage. Our children definitely need a balance. But more than anything, we need to recognize and affirm their place in our community, and their participation in the music of the parish can help foster their place in the parish family. It can contribute to the bonding of families and give them more ownership of the worship experience.

One of the ways this can be encouraged is for the religious educator and the parish music ministers to have a good working partnership. The music minister should make sure that the religious educator has access to the music that is part of the Sunday liturgy, so that the same music can be used in catechetical sessions, so that children can see the connection between worship and formation. Children should learn to sing the music they hear on Sunday. This is the music that should be primary in the religious education program, not music extracted from other sources. I am not saying that the liturgical music of the Sunday assembly should be the only source, but it should be held high as the major resource for the religious educator. Children can teach those of us who are adults. They hold their own wisdom that we need to learn from, and the language they can lead us with is certainly that of music.

Shaping the Music Ministers of Tomorrow

It is hoped that all of us recognize the importance of music in our Sunday liturgical celebrations, and the power that music has to enhance and give meaning to the worship experience for our people. If we believe this to be true, then we need to heed the responsibility that falls on us to be about the business of forming and training those who lead us in the musical ministries in the parish. In other words, if we do not have a process in place that forms the music ministers of tomorrow, then we are in danger of music being absent from our liturgies. And if that happens, the liturgy is less able to have the power to touch people. Liturgy is the source of the Christian life. It is where the community most seriously takes its call as the body of Christ. We need to instill a natural musicianship in our children so that those who possess the gift can come forward and answer the call to serve and strengthen the faith of God's people. If there is not good music, there is not good liturgy. And if there is not good liturgy, then our faith settles.

Music and Prayer

To be a Christian means to follow Jesus. To follow Jesus means to do what he did, to spread that message. I believe that Jesus was a singer. I am sure that he sang to people; he probably used music as a way to proclaim his message, and he invited those who encountered him to join in the song and dance of the Good News. The stories of Jesus need to be sung and shared with one another, and when children can sing the message, rather than just listen to someone else tell them about it, the message takes on a whole different level of meaning; children take on the presence of the Lord through their singing, movement, and gesture. They can become part of the story. More music needs to be composed and developed that can accomplish this. I realize that this is a challenge, but it is a very important and worthwhile challenge. The role of music in liturgy is to help people pray. Through music the child can experience Jesus rather than learn about the historical Jesus who lived a long time ago. Children need to know that Jesus lives with them now.

One of the problems in the passing on of our faith is that we give children and adults information rather than providing them an atmosphere where they can experience God in their lives. Music is primarily a language of the heart, not of the head. It presents wonderful possibilities for evangelizing our children. Through the language of song the children receive an experience of great joy. They can express their thanks, their fears, and their joys. Jesus said, "Let the little children come to me." Music provides a path for children to come to know the Lord, and in music, life can be found in the Lord.

Qualities Demanded of Music Ministers and Religious Educators

Many of the things I have presented here may seem overwhelming, impractical, or impossible, but I am speaking about a *dream*. If we do not dream, then we accomplish nothing. And we need to reflect on what this dream will require of the religious educator and the parish music minister.

More than anything, the persons entrusted with these responsibilites must *want* to give the gift of music to others. They must love the children and care for them, be on their side, and offer a welcome hand and heart. To work with students they need unbounded enthusiasm as well as intuitive powers and understanding. They must dare to be creative and spontaneous, and have the necessary resources and tools at hand—to have some basic fundamental musicianship, to understand at least the basic philosophies of various musical education movements, such as Kodaly and Orff. They must have a good understanding of Catholic Church music, and know the difference between liturgical music and music for performance. They must strive to empower the children to discover the musical spark—regardless of how advanced it may be—that is deep within them. These ministers must avoid using prepackaged methods from a textbook, but be able to adapt for the children involved. And they should have at least a minimal musical background, and if not, to at least have the sense and knowledge to know where to look for those who do have the skill. Musical snobs are not welcome here, for one must have an openness to all kinds and styles of music, to open up to children the many flavors that exist in the world of music.

And most important, they need creativity and the willingness to experiment, to take some chances. This aspect of music, which is so often neglected, should be strongly encouraged in the very beginning.

As I stated earlier, a lot of what I am sharing is a dream of mine, although I have been involved with many of these points and have learned from many successes and mistakes. I refuse to believe it can't be done. I am always trying to take some risks, to try something new. These issues are very important to me because I love music. I am a better person and a changed person because of music—it has enriched me and brought into my world many people, many insights, many gifts too numerous to mention. Once you have experienced something wonderful in your life, as I am sure all of you have at some time, it is impossible not to want to share it with everyone you can, to try to invite others to experience what you have experienced.

In my many years of working with children and young people, I have seen how music has made them better, how it has enriched their lives in the same way it has enriched mine. Because of music, I, and many of them, have come to experience a God of wonder and beauty, a God who loves us like no one else can love, a God who has, through this gift of music, filled our world with gifts unequaled. With all my heart I believe that music can enrich and give deeper meaning to the life of the church and to the mission that the Lord calls us to; to give the world a glimpse of Christ, a glimpse of the kingdom that will have all of us together like children gathered around a loving God.

Laura Bufano

FOURTEEN

MUSIC AND EDUCATION: THE SKY'S THE LIMIT

When the pastoral musician helps families and children pray together on a regular basis, the effects can spill over and nurture the growth of parish life and worship. Young people show a greater willingness to participate in larger parish celebrations. Choir membership increases. Families become more involved as they proudly support their children—sharing their gifts and talents with the parish family. Out of this involvement often comes the opportunity for spiritual growth and evangelization. The sky is the limit.

By working closely with directors of religious education and school administrators, a pastoral musician should establish contact with the children in the parish. Integration of large-group instruction into the religious education program and the school schedule (outside of the regular music program) would be ideal. This is aimed at preparing the children for active participation in prayer services and eucharistic liturgies. The musician needs to be constantly on the lookout for talented young people—singers, dancers, and instrumentalists—whose gifts could be developed and shared.

Pastoral musicians must become familiar with the Directory for Masses with Children and cooperate with religious educators who prepare liturgical celebrations for children—encouraging their creative efforts. Religious educators need support and guidance from the pastoral musicians with whom they are associated. By providing "in-service" days or workshops, pastoral musicians

121

and music educators can share their expertise and teaching strategies with religious educators.

The Religious Educator and Music

When religious educators are considering the integration of music into their religion class, they must first decide exactly what role they wish the music to play in a given lesson. Will the music be used to:

1. reinforce a concept that has already been presented in class?
2. introduce a new concept?
3. set a mood or create a particular atmosphere?
4. prepare a response or acclamation to be used in a forthcoming liturgical celebration?
5. break up the activity in a class?
6. get the children involved through movement?

Any of these objectives can be achieved through music, through any of the following means:

1. learning a new song;
2. singing a song that is already familiar to the children;
3. listening to a recording of other children singing;
4. responding rhythmically with their bodies to new music.

Some of these very experiences can later be transferred to a liturgical setting and become prayerful experiences as well. The key word is *preparation*, careful preparation on the part of the teacher. Long-range planning is an absolute requirement for music to be integrated successfully into religion classes.

When selecting songs, consideration should be given to the type of song chosen. Teachers should not choose only those songs that they like. In some instances, such songs may be inappropriate for children. Many of us tend to like what we know, and are often afraid to take the risk of learning something new. I encourage teachers to use the liturgical songs they already know as a springboard for integrating music into their religion classes. Then, I challenge them to risk and to explore the liturgical music resources that are available to them, and to learn something new.

After selecting a song, the teacher must listen to the recording several times. This listening serves a dual purpose: it helps the teacher to learn the song well and to find "teachable moments" in the song. It would be ideal for the teacher to memorize the song. These preliminary listenings enable the teacher to use creativity—planning the most effective teaching strategy for the song. Echo songs, songs with "catchy" refrains, songs with simple but tuneful melodies, songs that are rhythmically alive, and songs that easily lend themselves to dramatization or interpretative movement seem to work well with children of all ages.

Listening Strategies for Teaching Liturgical Music

Listening is an integral part of our particpation in any liturgical celebration. Whenever a song is presented, it should be heard once in its entirety, either sung by the teacher or played on a recording. It is important that the children get involved in the music immediately; simply tapping the beat silently during the first listening is sufficient. There should be no passive listening. The children ought to be given a focus—something to listen for each time the song is repeated. Very often, teachers are not comfortable with singing themselves. Therefore, the careful use of recordings can be a valuable tool in teaching liturgical music. Once a recording is being played and the volume is audible, I suggest that absolutely no talking be allowed in the room and that there be quiet listening on the part of the teacher as well as the children. This may sound too rigid for some readers, but in my experience it has had far-reaching positive results. If this routine is established, teachers and students are accountable to one another during silent listening and have the privilege of reminding one another when this rule is neglected. Young people, in particular, respond well to this shared responsibility. This ensures an atmosphere of quiet that is conducive to attentive and perceptive listening. Above all, it demonstrates a mutual respect for the music that is being heard. If a teacher needs to interrupt a listening session with some direction or comment, I would advise turning the volume to its softest level and, only then, speaking to the children. This practice encourages teachers to be prepared and to give simple but precise directions that can be easily understood by the children.

Interpretive Movement and Liturgical Music

Rarely do I teach a song to children without somehow using gesture and creative movement. The "kinesthetic" approach seems to deepen the learning experience for them and the songs become part of their beings.

There is no hard and fast rule that dictates whether children know a song completely before the gestures or interpretive movement is taught, nor is there any evidence defending the opposite approach that children learn the gestures first and then learn the melody and lyrics. The gestures for such songs as Joe Wise's "Come Out" and "His Banner Over Me" (found on several recordings) can be taught before the children have learned the text or the melody of the song. The process is simple; the teacher must have the song and the gestures memorized in order to present them effectively to the children. Children need to begin with the more structured prescribed movements of such songs as "Come Out" and "His Banner Over Me" before they can be expected to absorb and appreciate some of the movements suggested by songs that present abstract concepts. The song "Father, We Adore You" can become a simple, yet beautifully reverent movement prayer that children enjoy so much that they want to do it over and over again. At monthly family celebrations of the eucharist at Saint John the Evangelist Parish in New Hartford, New York, the entire congregation is invited to participate in the gestures to this acclamation. Young and old join in this movement prayer, and I assure you that they leave the church with smiling faces and joyful hearts.

Create your own movement prayers in song. It is not as difficult as it may at first seem. Because of the clear images in the text of some songs, they more easily lend themselves to interpretation than those songs whose meanings are more abstract. My suggestion is that you begin with songs that describe clear images. I firmly believe that the children can assist in creating movement and interpreting the lyrics of liturgical songs they know—transforming them into beautiful expressions of their faith. Suggestions for gestures and movements evolve gradually, after the children are sure of the melody and lyrics. First, there ought to be some discussion of the meaning of the song, and then suggestions could be made for signs and symbols that might convey the meaning. Taking a song one phrase at a time is the best approach. Each word or, in most instances, each phrase should be presented separately to the class and the suggestions could be made by the children for possible movements and gestures. Once a child makes a suggestion and demonstrates it, everyone in the class tries it, and if it works well, it is kept. If the idea does not work, the children in the class, with the teacher, refine the idea and if the originator of the idea approves, the gesture is used in the song in its revised form. When words, phrases, or concepts are repeated in a song, the use of the same gesture, or a variation on that gesture, not only creates unity in the composition, but also makes it easier for the children to remember.

I cannot overemphasize the importance of teaching a song gradually. It need not be taught in one lesson, and a teacher must use discretion in determining where to stop. The anticipation of continuing the learning process in the next class will heighten the awareness of the children, stimulate their interest, and foster enthusiasm. It is an enriching and powerful experience for the children to be able to share these movement prayers with their families and friends in a liturgical setting. What a joy!

Conclusion

Drawing from my own joyful and enriching experience working with children of various backgrounds and preparing them musically for liturgical and paraliturgical celebrations, I see a wealth of potential in religious educators who are willing to accept the challenge of integrating music into their religion classes. These teachers, as well as their students, will learn from one another—that is, teacher from students, students from teachers; and the growth which comes as a result of having embraced the challenge is immeasurable. I invite you—musicians and non-musicians as well—to implement some of the suggestions presented here, and if you are not immediately involved in working with children and liturgical preparation, encourage and support those who are involved. The rewards of such an endeavor will be great, and the joyful exuberance of young children when they are celebrating in song will speak for itself. Seeing the radiant expression on the face of one child who is caught up in the action of praying through gesture and song is a deeply moving experience. Teachers who dare to risk and invest part of themselves in teaching liturgical music creatively to children will discover that it is indeed a worthwhile investment. I dare you, then, to learn and to listen, to teach and to share, to discover and to create, You may surprise yourself.

FIFTEEN

SHOULD A MUSICIAN OFFER A RELIGIOUS EDUCATOR A HYMNBOOK?

Worship and religious education are two vital aspects of parish life: aspects that contribute to and nurture the growth of the life of faith. Parish religious education takes in so many age groups and interests that many parishes not only have a director of religious education (DRE), but also have coordinators for each segment of the religious education program.

"Fine," the parish musician might say, "but what does that have to do with me? My ministry is to the Sunday worshipers." True, the weekly gathering of our parish families to celebrate the eucharist is the focal point of the ministry of parish musicians. However, just as we are not "Sunday Catholics," neither can we, as parish musicians, be "Sunday ministers." Music is an integral expression of worship and religious growth. As musicians and liturgists we can help breathe musical life into this vital area of religious education.

Realizing the need for the contribution of the musician is the first step in the closer working relationship between the parish musician and DRE. In my work in religious education and liturgical music, I've found great similarity in ministries, and that's how it should be. All parish members are ultimately combining their efforts for the same goal: the deepening of our life together in the Lord. In some places though, one might think the opposite were true. Many groups (or individuals) work autonomously, duplicate efforts, and probably promote more frustration and exhaustion than peace and praise. However, the parish musician and the DRE working together and planning together can take a giant step to close this gap. What are some practical approaches the parish musician might take? What special contributions can the musician make in this area of parish life? Where does one begin?

The first step concerns our attitude as parish musicians and must be the basis of our endeavors. Ministry is to the total parish community, and so we must be willing to expand the horizons of the contributions we can make in the various phases of parish life. Since religious education is such an important ministry, the opportunity to consolidate efforts and make the wealth of our musical and liturgical resources available to the parish religious education program is essential.

This all sounds well and good, you might be thinking at this point, but becoming involved in religious education programs seems like an all encompassing job. First of all, I am not saying that the parish musician should function as music teacher for the religious education program. That could be too time-consuming; moreover, it is not really the role of the parish musician. The parish benefits more if the parish musician serves as a musical and liturgical resource person for the community's religious education program.

Input by Parish Staff

An essential beginning point is a meeting between the DRE and the parish musician. The purpose of this session would be to introduce the musician to the goals and basic thrust of the parish's religious education program. As a result of this first meeting, the parish musician should have a clear idea of the following: (1) the texts and any supplementary materials being used; (2) the main themes of each grade level; (3) the approach and format of the religious education sessions; and (4) sacramental programs: outlines of student and parent preparation, when the celebration of the sacraments is scheduled.

Another important meeting is with the religious education committee and clergy, especially when the committee is drawing up plans and schedule for the coming year. In this session the clergy, musician, DRE, school principal, and religious education committee select a top-priority area to concentrate on for the coming year. This is especially important to part-time musicians, since it provides an over-all program, establishes a priority area, and gives direction to the combined effort of available staff. In the long run, it makes the effort more fruitful for the entire parish.

A third important meeting would be with coordinators and staff. By "staff" I mean anyone involved in religious education: DRE, CCD and parochial school faculty, clergy, and coordinators. Staff will, of course, vary according to your parish structure. An effective initial contribution is made by sharing musical and liturgical expertise with this staff, including basic liturgical guidelines and an understanding of the appropriateness of music for worship and how music is an expression of faith. A working knowledge of Music in Catholic Worship (Bishops' Committee on the Liturgy) and the Directory for Masses with Children is essential. In this sharing session with coordinators and teachers, the parish musician can obtain clear ideas about music they've found to be expressive of their students' religious experiences. This exchange of ideas can serve as the basis for the next step.

Contributions by Parish Musician

When you know the basic thrust and themes of each level of the religious education program and take into consideration the suggestions of the DRE and teachers, you can then begin to offer ideas to the staff about music that will tie in with each group's particular topics. Music resources are known to the parish musician; but don't presume that because you know what's available, everyone else will know too. You might be surprised at the number of people who don't realize the sources (e.g., music, records, musicians) within their own parish. If the need arises for resources that the parish does not have, the parish musician can at least make known where these can be found. Diocesan liturgy and religious education offices are usually well-stocked with a variety of appropriate materials.

Encourage religious education teachers to seek out musical talent in their own classes. Many times we overlook the "living resources" in our midst. The more the students can contribute and participate, the more integral will be the musical expression to their religious experience. Music is not an attention-getting gimmick, nor should it be something "tacked on" at the end of a class. When a class is planning a special celebration and they have insufficient musical talent in their own group, the parish musician could arrange for some members of the parish guitar group or the children's choir to facilitate their musical prayer. In a case like this, however, it is extremely important that the small group truly pray with all present and not be there as "performers." Their presence at one of the planning sessions for the service is essential.

Sacramental preparation is a hub around which many parish religious education programs revolve. The prayerful and practical preparation of parents and children for their on-going participation in sacramental life can be overwhelming if left to one or two people. This is the opportunity for the clergy, parish musician, religious education faculty and committee to do their utmost in a cooperative effort.

The parish musician's contribution is much more than rehearsing the hymns a few times with the group concerned. Early planning of sacramental celebrations is necessary so that the basic themes of the sacraments, clearly understood by the planners, áre integrated into the people's experiences. Have you ever witnessed the disaster of a celebration that didn't really spring from the experience of the group that was supposed to be celebrating? Undoubtedly this could have been avoided by better and/or earlier planning and better knowledge of musical resources. It is the responsibility of the parish musician to participate in *early* planning and to make the best possible musical resources available for both sacramental preparation and celebration.

After the planning stage, the parish musician should also be incorporated into the sacramental preparation sessions. People must be comfortable with the music for it to be a true prayer form.

Obviously, all this cannot be done at once. The pace and direction of your combined efforts will greatly depend on the circumstances of your own parish. These few initial steps for parish musicians and religious education staff members may assist in a more effective ministry.